HER STORY

HER STORY

*Essays on the
Goddess in Our Lives*

ANNABEL LINDY

SOWILO PRESS
Philadelphia 2010

Copyright © 2010 by The Estate of Annabel Lindy

All rights reserved

No part of this book may be used or reproduced in any manner whatsoever without written permission, except in the case of brief quotations embodied in critical articles and reviews.

Library of Congress Control Number: 2010902348
ISBN 978-0-9844727-0-3

Credits for the images appear on page 231.

SOWILO PRESS
An imprint of Hidden River Publishing
P.O. Box 421
Bala Cynwyd, PA 19004, USA

CONTENTS

Preface *vii*

1 ❖ Once upon a Time *1*
2 ❖ The Missing Years *12*
3 ❖ Mountain Mother *25*
4 ❖ The Judgment of Paris *34*
5 ❖ The Lady of the Moon *43*
6 ❖ The Dark Goddess *54*
7 ❖ Making the World Go Round *67*
8 ❖ The Story of Oedipus *79*
9 ❖ From the World of Milk and Honey *87*
10 ❖ Pots and Cauldrons *98*
11 ❖ Way of the Way *108*
12 ❖ The Double Axe *122*
13 ❖ Blood and Sacrifice *133*
14 ❖ Rebirth of the Sun *145*
15 ❖ The New Year Festival *154*
16 ❖ The Sacred Stones *164*
17 ❖ Sacred Dance *176*
18 ❖ The Energies of the Earth *185*
19 ❖ Tragedy *197*
20 ❖ Water *208*
21 ❖ The Dawning of the Age of Aquarius *219*

PREFACE

I HAVE BEEN RESEARCHING AND WRITING ABOUT THE Goddess cultures since the 1990s, after discovering a world that made sense—where history, anthropology, and Jungian psychology come together.

Through my life, I've been a businesswoman, housewife, mother, and grandmother, descended from three generations of strong women. My passion for this study led to travel around the world. Visits to such places as Carnac, Newgrange, Avebury, Stonehenge, Greece, Crete, and Israel have enriched my understanding of this subject matter.

I dedicate this work to the friends and family who have encouraged me, and most especially to the younger generation of women who deserve to know what I have learned.

HER STORY

CHAPTER 1

Once upon a Time

ONCE UPON A TIME, A LONG, LONG TIME AGO, HUMANS had a very different way of seeing themselves, their community, and their relationship to the world and the universe. This was the period of time back at the very beginning of civilization during the Old Stone Age, around 30,000 BCE, and moving forward to the time when Father Abraham left Ur, around 2000 BCE. In this world, the deity was female. At that time, as Elinor Gadon in *The Once and Future Goddess*, tells us, "the ancient Goddess cultures were woman-centered, peaceful and egalitarian," which is certainly different from ours.

According to Elinor Gadon, the "Goddess religion was earth-centered, not heaven-centered, of this world not other-worldly, body-affirming not body-denying, holistic not dualistic.... The religious quest was above all for renewal, for the regeneration of life, and the Goddess was the life force." The major religious focus was expressed through the awe felt toward the power of the female to create life. Today we have lost this wonder the ancients felt towards the creation of life. However, even then, the fertility of women was only part of the religious expression.

The ancients of this era saw birth and death as part of an ongoing and continuing energy cycle moving constantly in the spiral of birth to death to birth again. All the cycles of the world, night to day to night, summer to winter to summer, were included and seen as proof and instances of the basic cycle of life. I think it helps to remember they thought of the deity, the Great Goddess, as containing the whole cycle within Herself. Remember, the whole cycle had many aspects, each one of which was only a part of the whole. In addition to the power to bring and take life, other aspects of the Great Goddess include the creation of all the arts of civilization such as healing, writing, mathematics, music and the giving of just law. As Riane Eisler in *The Chalice and the Blade* says "It was a world very different from ours in that there was no separation between the ordinary and the sacred. Religion was life and life was religion."

While Eric Neumann, in *The Great Mother*, uses the term "Great Mother" to describe the deity, Marija Gimbutas, in *The Language of the Goddess*, finds this description too limiting. She prefers, and feels her archeological research supports, the title of Great Goddess who alone gave and took life. The power of the Great Goddess was revealed in the existence of water, stone, caves, springs, animals, bees, birds, snakes, fishes, hills, trees, graves and flowers. These objects were seen as manifestations of the Great Goddess; and the ancients believed She lived in these objects. These beliefs are found all through the ancient world. Eisler suggests that one possible explanation for the remarkable religious unity that existed could be that the "Goddess appears to have been originally worshiped in all ancient agricultural societies."

Early humans considered all these above-mentioned transformations as magical and sacred. According to Neumann, transformation symbolism always became sacral when it ceased to be a natural process and was changed by human activity. Such acts as baking, wine or beer making, weaving and spinning by this definition are sacred. Certainly this gives a different spin to what has been known as the value of woman's work. These transformations were not seen as we would see them today, as a mere technical process, but were seen as a sacred mystery.

In this world, there was an ongoing continuation of energy cycles forming and dissolving. This constant energy is displayed in the movement expressed in the art. The ceramics, in particular, display dynamic motion with bold strong patterns of whirling spirals and coiling snakes which show the energy of the cycles of life displayed by the Great Goddess. Hanging on the walls where I bank are large tapestries woven with these very same patterns. They fascinate me each time I'm there. Also I can remember visiting St. Mark's Cathedral in Venice. Almost everyone was involved with viewing the wonderful art work on the walls and ceilings. But I had just finished Gimbutas's book, so I found the mosaics on the floor, identical to what she had described as being symbols of the Great Goddess, to be even more fascinating. Today we call such artwork abstract or geometric. In ancient days such work expressed reverence to the Great Goddess.

Doubt has been expressed about the existence of the Goddess culture. But archeological evidence, the surviving bits and pieces of tales and legends, the words decoded from ancient tablets, the abundance of artwork and ceramics all tell us these societies really existed. Not only did they exist, but the data tells us it was a peaceful world. War as we know it did not occur. The world that created the viewpoint which honored all the cycles of life and nature was a world surprisingly peaceful. People worked together, lived comfortably (in some places even with indoor plumbing) and celebrated their lives with beautiful artwork, ceramics, dance and music. It was also a world very different from ours where harmony reigned, and there was no separation between the ordinary and the sacred. Not until the late Neolithic or early Bronze Age were there fortifications around the villages, or did grave artifacts include weapons.

Over the centuries, all of the rich life of this ancient world was lost to us. It is only with the development of the field of archeology and with the scholars' increased understanding of the ancient languages that we are able to uncover the story of those ancient times. Today we know more about this era than anyone has ever known at any other time in history.

Barbara Walker, in *The Woman's Encyclopedia of Myths and Secrets*, tells us that during the Neolithic Age "the matrilineal clan system and the rule of mother-right were followed almost everywhere." The communities of the Great Goddess were matrilineal, which means descent and inheritance was passed through the women. In matrilineal communities, the main tie was a mother and her children. A mother would pass her wealth to her daughters, while a father would pass his wealth not to his children, but to his sister's children. In this community, inheritance as well as descent was through the mother, and the tribal elders were menopausal women. Amazing, isn't it? It sounds odd to us, but it is just a different way to cut the pie. Since we now have the laws of various ancient communities, we know how this process worked.

Robert Graves in *The Greek Myths* says that in the earliest days of human life on Earth no gods existed. The Great Goddess was regarded as immortal, changeless and omnipotent: and the concept of fatherhood had not been introduced into religious thought. She took lovers, but for pleasure, not to provide her children with a father. Men feared, adored, and obeyed the matriarch; the hearth which she tended in a cave or hut was their earliest social center, and motherhood was their prime mystery.

It is important for us not to think of these societies as being structured similarly to ours, merely dominated by women instead of men. That doesn't appear to have been the structure at all. Riana Eisler tells us that, "both men and women worked together in equal partnership for the common good." The attitude seems to have been a linking rather than a ranking of the sexes. Eisler then goes on to say that, although it is likely that priestesses primarily officiated at the worship of the Goddess, there is also evidence of participation of a priest. This is supported by the images of the bull and the bullhorns, which have a central place in many Neolithic shrines and later in Minoan imagery. According to Gimbutas "neither sex is subordinate to the other; by complementing one another, their power is doubled." From the earliest societies, we have found artifacts and art to indicate that males played a strong role in the society, but not a dominant one.

The geographic area which this concept governed was vast. It included all of Old Europe down through the Middle East into India and at least Egypt. Throughout these areas an enormous number of artifacts have been found which demonstrate the power of the Great Goddess. In addition, early ancient writers, the Sumerians and Greeks for example, report events and activities that related to this period. Each passing year, as archeologists keep discovering more artifacts, we are able to add to our knowledge. Recent advancements in our understanding of the languages of those times permit greater opportunities for decoding the large number of ancient tablets. These tablets cover the entire range of civilized activity, from poetry to trade arrangements and legal procedures.

It is this ancient era which produced the images of females with large breasts and buttocks, sometimes in the act of giving birth, sometimes pregnant, and sometimes pointing or holding their breasts. Scholars say these figures are the earliest representation of the Great Goddess. The patriarchal world, completely missing the point, calls them "Venus figures." One of the best known of these figures is the Earth Mother of Willendorf created about 30,000–25,000 years ago and found in Austria.

The Venus of Laussel (left) and the Venus of Willendorf

Another from this very early period is the Goddess of Laussel, a rock carving from 22,000–18,000 BCE in the Dordogne of France.

The time of the Great Goddess extended over many thousands of years from the time of the painted caves around 30,000 BCE or even earlier until about 3500 BCE. How humans thought of her changed over this time period. At first She ruled alone. Alone, She gave birth to the world; and all of the world's creatures were born from Her body. Most of the world's creation stories start this way. As time went on, the imagery and stories changed. The Goddess no longer created life alone, but now united with a god. Since these were agricultural communities, the god was a vegetable god, which meant he died each year at the end of each growing season, as did the crops. For the crops to grow again the next season, the ancients felt the land must be renewed. The ceremony which was absolutely necessary to provide the renewal, called for the Goddess to mate with a God in what the Greeks called a *Hieros Gamos*, a "sacred marriage." Barbara Walker tells us the sacred marriage was one of the main rituals of the ancient world. The priestess/queen was the goddess and the priest/king took the role of the god. Archeologists have found numerous ancient seals and plaques portraying this ritual of the sacred marriage. In addition, we have from different geographic areas, the traditional poems which were read at the proper times of the year in the temples to celebrate the sacred marriage. There are scholars who feel the biblical Song of Songs described such a sacred marriage. I always wondered how such an erotic hymn made its way into the Bible.

While so far, the world before the Iron Age seems idyllic, it is best to remember that of the various rituals and festivals used to mark the cycles of time, one of the most important was the annual ritual sacrifice of the king. There are many theories as to why ancient communities made this a central ritual. They range from the agricultural society's involvement with the crops cycle, to a belief that primitive humans felt killing an animal or pulling crops from the soil was a violation of the Great Goddess for which atonement was necessary. Although the Latin definition for sacrifice means "to make whole or sacred," remember Latin was developed many centuries after the ritual was developed. The concept must have existed long before. The literature is full of myths and stories of the king being put to death, either at a fixed time or at the first sign of bodily decay.

After the king was sacrificed, custom required a new king to be chosen. To the ancients this represented rebirth in the vegetable world. In earliest times, the choice was made by the priestess, as stand-in for the Great Goddess. The choice was usually the winner of some event such as a race or archery contest. A variation, of course, would be that the person who slew the old king became the new king. But however he was chosen, a king only became the king by entering into the *Hieros Gamos* with the queen/priestess. In these early cultures the king ruled only if the Goddess or her earthly personage accepted him. This ceremony of the ancient world is what made the king the king. Even today, this is the ancient ritual performed which makes the emperor of Japan a God. Early men had no ruling power in their own right; their kingship came from being a consort to the queen/priestess.

Another view of why ritual killing became so important relates to the waning and disappearance of the moon. The cycle of decrease, disappearance and then reappearance may have created the idea that death was necessary to re-energize life. This idea is supported by the myth of Osiris, The Egyptian God of Vegetation, who brought farming to the Egyptians and who was murdered by his brother Set. This was a common theme in the Neolithic period. The stories of Attis, Adonis and Tammuz tell of these other young gods being sacrificed. According to Sjoo and Mor, their stories are pretty much the same. They are all Vegetation Gods who were ritually sacrificed, usually on a tree. Their flesh was eaten as bread, their blood drunk as wine. This ritual sacrifice, conducted in the harvest season, was believed to be necessary for the land's fertility.

Whatever the reason, the king (or king acting as god) was killed. At first the event took place annually or possibly semi-annually, but as time went on and the power of the Great Goddess began to diminish a bit, the kings were able to develop ways to avoid the event or at least arrange for it to happen less frequently, or for it to happen to someone else entirely. Eventually, the sacrificial body became that of an animal, which brings us down in time to the Romans.

What happened to break down the Great Goddess systems? The possibilities offered depend on whose material you're studying. Neumann, the Jungian, says as humans developed they acquired larger personal egos, which created a need for humans to separate from the unity of the Great Mother (Neumann's term). So they created new deities to represent their growing egos. Other writers, such as Gerda Lerner or Riane Eisler (usually, but not necessarily feminist writers and scholars) say it was just another example of men being oppressive to women. Historians suggest that waves of invaders came in from the steppes of Russia. These invaders, called Aryans or Indo-Europeans, spoke a common language, worshipped male gods, and through their superior military skills and weapons, conquered the Great Goddess communities. Then as conquerors do, they imposed their own values. You can choose any or all of the above. Personally, I like the historical wave approach. However, it is not useful in explaining to me why the Aryans had their patriarchal gods and system in the first place. Gimbutas claims it was because they were pastoralists, who in their dealing with herds of goats and cows developed weapons and a need for the superior strength of men. The discussion is still open.

Regardless of the theories, it is historically true that Aryans came and conquered. At first, the change was gradual because they blended in with the local conquered populations. It is important to remember the older communities were both more comfortable and more civilized than the hard riding and rough world of the Aryans. But by 1300 BCE or so, the conquering hordes completely took over. The world of the Goddess was destroyed. The most common way of marking the change from a female god to a male god was for the new father god to participate in a "sacred marriage" with the old goddess. The child of this union would then create a new form. This is why in Greek mythology, the new father god Zeus is so busy seducing the various local deities, such as Leda or Europa. Each of these females was the local goddess for a conquered community.

In spite of the invaders' best efforts, most cultures managed to bury a large layer of ancient beliefs and practices under the patriarchy. The world of the Great Goddess did not die.

She and Her traditions went underground. The imagery was debased and distorted but not completely destroyed. What in the old tradition had been valued was held by the new in contempt. The symbols were twisted, the stories were changed, but what once was sacred could not easily be dismissed. Country folk still, on some level, believed and used the ancient symbols from the Goddess in areas such as sacred wells, springs, holy trees and groves, and with good luck charms to cure infertility and such. Our fairy tales and many of our seasonal holidays also hark back to the early days. Humans and human emotions haven't changed much, even over the passing of many thousands of years. Jungians would say that this is because all modern people have within them the symbols and beliefs of all the civilizations that have gone before. They call this the "collective unconscious."

According to the Jungians, when we dream it is the ancient symbols and images which come to us. Because we dream in these images, and because we still use them in our art, our stories, and our rituals to express basic concepts, they still strongly affect us. Since in so many cases the symbols have been distorted, we no longer understand them. This means that we have lost a powerful connection to our inner life.

FOR FURTHER READING

Baring, Anne, and Cashford, Jules. *The Myth of the Goddess.* New York: Penguin, 1991. Print.

Christ, Carol P., and Plaskow, Judith, Editors. *Womanspirit Rising.* San Francisco: Harper & Row, 1979. Print.

Eisler, Riane. *The Chalice and the Blade.* New York: Harper & Row, 1988. Print.

Frazer, Sir James George. *The Golden Bough.* New York: Macmillan, 1922. Print.

Gadon, Elinor W. *The Once and Future Goddess.* New York: HarperCollins, 1989. Print.

Gimbutas, Marija. *The Language of the Goddess.* New York: Harper & Row, 1989. Print.

Neumann, Erich. *The Great Mother.* Princeton, NJ: Princeton University Press, 1963. Print.

Lerner, Gerda. *The Creation of Patriarchy.* Oxford, England: Oxford University Press, 1986. Print.

Sjoo, Monica, and Mor, Barbara. *The Great Cosmic Mother.* New York: Harper & Row, 1987. Print.

Walker, Barbara. *The Woman's Dictionary of Symbols & Sacred Objects.* San Francisco: Harper & Row, 1988. Print.

———. *The Woman's Encyclopedia of Myths and Secrets.* San Francisco: Harper & Row, 1983. Print.

CHAPTER 2

The Missing Years

TIME IS THE REAL PROBLEM, OR RATHER OUR LACK OF understanding of the vastness of it. I feel, for instance, that most of us in the Western World share the idea that the patriarchs of the Bible came from a very early time and they created from scratch, so to speak, the traditions and customs we find in the early books of the Bible. In reality, that is just not true. Scholars date Moses to about 1300 BCE (Before the Common Era) and from there they work back to Abraham living at about 1800 BCE. These dates are very approximate, because nothing really checks out exactly. However, these are the dates usually given. Now, 1800 BCE is less than 4,000 years ago. Granted, that is a long time. But since the Ice Age ended around 12,000 years ago, which permitted the development of agriculture and the start of town life, we are missing about 8,000 years of human life and activity. What this means is that when Abraham left Ur, he traveled with a complete stock of ancient customs, traditions, law, poetry, mythology and history that go back into the period of time we usually skip.

Only in the last century or so have we been able to uncover much material from these missing 8,000 years. Since writing had not yet been developed, most of what we are learning comes from archeological information. If you add to this the legends and myths that go back into antiquity, there is now a considerable amount of available information, more than has ever existed before.

Myths and legends as basic sources of information are difficult, because it is hard to decipher what is original and what has been added through time. Scholars get very upset with ideas they are unable to firmly establish. Yet with the amount of information already available, patterns can be established. Some archeologists have been leaders in working with the patterns to establish a sense of the ancient world. Marija Gimbutas, the archeologist, is certainly in the lead here.

Gimbutas tells us that a relatively new source of validation for these new interpretations of archeological findings comes from the followers of C. G. Jung. The Jungians explore the dreams of their patients to heal and cure. Much of their work in dream interpretation involves exploring what they call the "collective unconscious," which is the collection of symbols and archetypes we humans use to express and personify our feelings and which, according to the Jungians, each member of the human race inherits along with all the other attributes that make us human. For explanations of what these symbols mean, they look to ancient poetry, imagery and mythology. Many would consider this only speculation and wild guessing concerning material before written history; but Jungians point to the dreams and artwork of their patients, which matches the imagery of the ancient world. So, if you are willing to consider the Jungian explanations, much more material can be added to help explore life during the missing years.

First though, we have to go very far back into time, to the Ice Age 50,000 to 30,000 years ago, when the massive ice fields covering Europe and Asia started to melt. Anne Baring and Jules Cashford, in *The Myth of the Goddess*, tell us how this changed the world. Before then, it was so cold that few animals could live on the frozen ground. As Europe began to warm, the ground became less frozen. First, grassland and then forests grew. Finally, during this period, animals came into the area followed by the first humans like us, *Homo sapiens*, named the Cro-Magnons. They were named after the locality in which moderns first discovered them. They were hunters who followed the animals. Some found homes near the entrances of what we today call the painted caves of southwestern France. Rachel Gertrude Levy tells us in *Gate of Horn* that these Cro-Magnon humans left records of the development of a system of beliefs and practices which, although they have been lost and changed through the many later civilizations, may be shown to have influenced and helped create the spiritual and intellectual activities of today. Central to their beliefs and practices is the concept of the deity being a Mother goddess.

The Cro-Magnons were a tall and well-proportioned people with a brain capacity like that of modern man. Their stone implements are distributed across Europe and the Near East. Alexander Marshack tells us in *The Roots of Civilization* that they had considerable knowledge. They had knowledge not only of the sky, the seasons, and animals but also of materials and processes. They knew the quality and uses of hide, bone, antler, fat, coal, charcoal, wood, fire, stone, and had an extremely varied and useful tool kit. They knew the varieties of stone, the various plants, the colors of charcoal, oxides, and clays, and the technical processes of decoration on body, bone, stone, and shelter or cave wall. They knew how to make structures, huts, pits, nets, fireplaces and drainage ditches. They knew the varied uses of story and the symbolic uses of magic, ceremony, and music. They also had a range of uses for fire, from diverse forms of cooking, to the hardening of clay figures, to the use of oil lamps for lighting shelters and caves. They were hardly the ignorant cave men of our stories and comics.

As part of their culture, they painted extraordinary paintings on the walls deep inside the limestone caves of the area;

many of the paintings are huge. According to Ann Sieveking, in *The Cave Artists*, they painted mainly animals, some human forms, handprints and symbols. It was also here that they carved their many female statues. These were left as a record of their lives, which covered at least 15,000 years, from 30,000 to 15,000 BCE, of the Paleolithic (Old Stone) Age. The scholarship of Gertrude Rachel Levy, Marija Gimbutas, and Vincent Scully, among others, tells us that these creations were meant by the ancients to invoke the Goddess, in all of her aspects and powers. Baring and Cashford refer to the hollowed shape of the cave as the womb of the Mother Goddess and tell us that these caves tell the story of the great primeval Goddess through the art and rituals that took place inside them. It seems the early humans of this period considered the cave as the womb from which humans were born and to which the dead returned.

There are more than 200 painted caves in France and Spain alone, a large percentage of which have been discovered only in the last 100 years. In December of 1994, I read of a newly-discovered cave in the south of France which contained over 300 wall paintings. Radiocarbon tests revealed that the images were more than 30,000 years old; that makes this the oldest cave yet known. The drawings suggest a technical skill and art tradition which reveal "primitive" man as a gifted and imaginative artist.

In spite of my claustrophobia, I loved visiting some fifteen of these painted caves. We started at Altamira in Spain where the most magnificent bulls are painted on the cave ceiling, and worked from there to the Cougnac caves and Lascaux II in the Dordogne in France. It was a glorious experience, and I learned so much.

While each cave was unique, they all seemed to follow the same general style. For each of them, we followed winding, narrow and naturally dark passages in and down. Making this trip only with flashlights to relieve the blackness gave the word "dark" a whole new meaning. I felt I was having a 20th century primal experience. To the ancients, in a world where everything was magic and sacred, it had to be an overwhelming experience. Erich Neumann, in *The Great Mother*, says the dark and danger of the journey into the deep interior of the caves was fundamental to the cave experience. Deep inside, the walls are covered with wonderful paintings of animals. These awesome paintings were made around 25,000 BCE to 15,000 BCE. They were done by people who had imagination, traditions and skill, as well as the ability to express their inner thoughts and feelings through paint, sculpture and carved artifacts. Scholars have spent their professional lives trying to sort out the meanings of the artwork. While there are many theories, nothing is sure.

In the over 200 caves of Spain and France, more than 130 statues of women, always naked, generally small, and often pregnant were discovered. Most of them have the look of mothers. To call these figures "fertility figures," as some do, dismisses their power. The Jungians Baring and Cashford feel calling them "Mother Goddess" or simply "Goddess" restores their original dignity. These figures are of the Goddess who represented the life-giving, nourishing and regenerating powers of the universe.

In these figures, Baring and Cashford see evidence of the beginning of the later Mother Goddess worship found in the communities of the Bronze Age. They find here many of the Bronze Age images, which include giving birth, offering nourishment from the breast, and receiving the dead back into the womb for rebirth. These same images appear throughout the art of human history. All express a similar vision of life on Earth, one in which the creative source of life is expressed by the image of a Mother, where humanity feels itself and the rest of creation to be Her children. These same images occur in the Old Stone Age, as they do 10,000 years later in the New Stone Age, and 5,000 years after that in the Bronze and Iron ages.

Also in the caves, the Goddess, as the source of life, was frequently shown abstractly in the shape of a triangle. Elinor Gadon, in *The Once and Future Goddess*, feels the triangle is a natural symbol to represent the vulva from which life emerges, and that it also represents sacred power. Sometimes this would be carved on the pubic area of the figure; sometimes the triangle representing the vulva would stand alone. In France alone, there are more than 100 images of this vulva from the Paleolithic Age. I'm always reminded of these triangles when I see young women working out at the gym, wearing brightly colored bikini bottoms over their workout outfits. They look just like the carvings on the statues. The idea of the triangle was so widespread throughout the world that I wasn't even surprised when, recently, I saw the carved pubic triangles on pictures of five thousand year old statues found in Ecuador.

No one knows exactly what happened to the cave dwellers or their culture; but, since over the thousands of years, the climate kept growing warmer, maybe they just left the caves. Baring and Cashford suggest that, around 12,000–10,000 BCE, the people who lived in the caves would leave them for the seasonal hunt, and then come back for winter. As the weather warmed, they started to build summer dwellings. Eventually, they began to settle and sow seeds of grain, in time leaving the cave completely. Whatever happened, after 15,000 BCE, to our knowledge, no one lived in the painted caves anymore. Baring and Cashford tell us that the 2,000 to 3,000 years which elapsed from the end of life in the caves to the creation of the communities in the river valleys of Old Europe is not long, when you consider the immense time span of the earlier period.

What is amazing is that the same ritual structures and images of the goddess are found as far apart as Britain and Malta, Old Europe and Anatolia. The picture emerging is that of the existence of a single cultural idea which connected all these areas. We don't know if this was one culture which spread over the whole world, or if it was that humans in the same stage of development developed the same ideas to express their beliefs and feelings. When people from this period traveled, they might not have understood the languages of the new places, but the meaning of the religious imagery in the new communities would be clear because, at this stage, the goddess was universally worshipped.

The next communities we know of emerged around 6500 BCE, in the river valleys of Eastern Europe. Gimbutas excavated this culture, which she called "Old Europe." It covered the area from the Aegean and Adriatic Seas, as far north as Czechoslovakia, southern Poland, and the western Ukraine. The people of this area formed settlements, which were of a good size, involving craft specialization and the creation of religious and governmental institutions. According to Gimbutas, this culture was pre-Indo-European and matrilineal. She writes that the focus of this culture was the figure of a goddess who was the source and giver of all.

The Old Europe communities were made up of farmers who grew wheat, barley, peas and other beans. All the domesticated animals except the horse were used. They utilized copper and gold for ornaments and tools and seemed even to have developed a rudimentary script. Trading ranged over large areas through the seas and inland waterways.

Baring and Cashford tell us that there were some 3,000 Old Europe sites from which archeologists have found about 30,000 miniature sculptures made of clay, marble, bone, copper and gold. They also found vast numbers of ritual vessels, shrines, altars and implements of sacrifice, painted vases, inscribed objects, as well as clay models of temples. What I find hard to believe is that until these excavations were done, all of this complex civilization was unknown.

These communities seem to have enjoyed peace as well as prosperity, for there is no sign of any invasions in their communities. Providing protection against enemies was not needed until later. A hill or mountain site was chosen for a shrine, not for a citadel or fortified camp. During this early period the deities carry no emblems associated with might, such as spears, swords or thunderbolts. There are no pictures that celebrate or even depict war. Rather, the images are from nature, and show feeling for the beauty and sanctity of life. Since scholars assumed that the people who lived so long ago were quite primitive, they had difficulty accepting how old, yet sophisticated, these communities were.

These communities used a whole series of symbols—spirals, chevrons, zigzags, meanders and net-like patterns—which cover many of the artifacts traditionalists call "geometric decorations." Gimbutas sees in them a written language. She calls it "an alphabet of the metaphysical." According to her, each pattern displays a different aspect of the Goddess's powers. While I am amazed by museums which still label these patterns "geometric decorations," according to Gimbutas, if you do not recognize the important unifying quality of the Great Goddess this is an easy mistake to make.

The Old Europe culture which Gimbutas evacuated existed some 5,000–6,000 years before the age of Classical Greece. Elinor Gadon tells us the dominant motif of Old European symbolism was regeneration, the maintenance of life. With the development of agriculture, grain became the sacrament. The sacred female from the Painted Caves now became the Vegetation Goddess in Old Europe. In time she will evolve into Demeter, the Grain Goddess of Greece.

As early as 7000 BC there were other isolated centers of this European culture in places as separated as Eastern Europe, southern Turkey, Egypt, Palestine, Mesopotamia, and the Indus Valley. Almost identical figurines and sculptures of the Goddess have been found in many of these far-flung places. What is most amazing is that the same ritual structures and images of the goddess are found in ancient civilizations all over Europe, the Near East and down to India. These are the civilizations that laid the foundations of architecture, astronomy, mathematics, writing and cultural relations in places we always believed were too primitive to be considered. This means, as Baring and Cashford tell us, we must give up our idea of primitive tribes lurking in the darkness of pre-history awaiting our civilized minds to enlighten them. We also lose the right to use the condescending terminology of "idols," "Venus figures" and "fertility cults."

In the Near East, the agricultural settlements began around 12,000 years ago at the time of the development of agriculture and the domestication of animals. Gadon tells us that the largest of these Neolithic cities, Catal Huyuk in southern Anatolia (now modern Turkey), is the earliest known culture documenting the Goddess. Catal Huyuk was discovered in 1927 by James Mellaart. This community thrived from 7000 to 5000 BCE, when for some unknown reason the site was deserted.

In Catal Huyuk we find many splendors, among them groups of sanctuaries and shrines, decorated with wall paintings, plaster reliefs, animal heads, and cult statues. The mood is joyful, the dominant themes celebrating the renewal of life. There, some 3,000 years before the rise of Sumeria, artisans were already doing highly skilled craft work including such things as stone carving, weaving, cloth dyeing, pottery, basket work, spinning, and the construction of houses and shrines. Peg Streep in *Sanctuaries of the Goddess* tells us the city traded with regions farther south, as the discovery of cowry shells from the Red Sea and dentalium, whelks, and cockles from the Mediterranean attest. Bowls, cosmetic palettes, axes of greenstone, and other objects reflect sophisticated techniques of grinding and polishing stone. Out of 139 living rooms excavated, at least forty and probably more, appear to have served a religious function. These cult rooms or shrines are more elaborately decorated than the houses, and frequently but not always, they are the largest buildings in the quarter.

Baring and Cashford say that in Catal Huyuk the central religious image was the Mother Goddess, who appears in three aspects: young woman, mother giving birth and old woman. In the shrines she was sculpted in relief and painted on the walls. The main theme in many of the shrines was the physical act of birth. The Mother Goddess of Catal Huyuk sits on a rock-like throne, resting her hands on animals by her side in the act of giving birth. If this sounds familiar don't be surprised, as this image of the Goddess with her guardian lions appears again and again in later periods. Figures of the Goddess as Inanna-Istar from Mesopotamia, Isis and Sedhmet in Egypt and the unnamed Minoan Goddess all walk with, or are on top of lions or sit on a lion throne. In Roman times Cybele, the Great Goddess of Rome, rides in a chariot drawn by lions. The later Goddess and the lion motif descend directly from the goddess of Catal Huyuk.

In Britain a major visual example from the Neolithic period (8000 BCE–4000 BCE) of the Goddess ruling alone is Silbury Hill, a mammoth manmade hill in England, over 130 feet high, which just sits there. I was awed by its power. When I saw it, the guide said scholars could not discover why it was built. At first they thought it was a burial tomb as are the pyramids in Egypt, but they couldn't find evidence of any burial chambers. He said it had been photographed, probed and investigated, but nothing was inside. He invited us to climb it, but since it was raining, we declined. That, I realized later, was a great mistake. From the flattened top of the hill, you can see that the hill itself is a large pregnant belly, while the moat dug around is in the shape of a woman's body squatting in the ancient birthing position. Scholars say during the full moon at the time of the summer harvest, the rising moon was reflected in the water of the moat, so it looked like a child's head being born. The Goddess is giving birth to the moon. Folk custom from the area suggests this might have been the signal to the community to start reaping the harvest. I wish I could have seen this ritual, as it must have been some sight.

Baring and Cashford explain that, since originally all things were part of the Great Mother, she embodied both male and female attributes. Since they are Jungians, their explanation of what happened is that the evolution of consciousness created a breakdown of what was once experienced as one. It seems that around the seventh and sixth millennia BCE the Goddess who was one in Old Europe separates into female and male elements, the male becoming the fertilizing power and the female the gestating womb. The male principle is shown as the phallus, as the bull or horned animal—ram and goat—and as the serpent. The image of the god appears about the same time in Old Europe as in Catal Huyuk. These symbols of the male principle show up all through both areas. This is certainly supported by all of the bullhorns as well as phalluses and boars found in the sites.

Of course the young god, the son-consort of the Goddess, makes his appearance at this same time as a recurring part in the central miracle of pre-patriarchal religion, the mystery of regeneration and rebirth. Baring and Cashford tell us that he may be shown as the reaper of corn or perhaps the corn itself, which is cut down and reborn in the annual cycle of agriculture. He may then also personify the god of the yearly cycle, who is "cut down" with the passing of the year, yet at the same time reborn as the new year.

While the idea of the Goddess was a unifying idea, cultures could develop certain ideas of her as they chose. She was different things to different people. Nothing can destroy her, for she has no substantial existence. She was an idea, a projection which comes from our own dearest wishes and longed-for desires and greatest fears. This is why the Jungians say she is still within each of us.

As time went on, for a variety of reasons, conquest being only one of them, the power of the single Great Mother diminished. Jungians say as humans evolved, they felt restricted by the smothering demands of her power. Think of a two-year-old beginning to pull away from the power of mother. Humans felt less like the children of the mother and needed new forms to express themselves. Eventually, the ancient culture was lost. It is only now through archeology we have been able to add to our knowledge a small piece of the lost matriarchal world.

So when we are told that our society, the system we have now—with its warlike, domineering, violent ways—is the way it always has been, 20,000 years of the rule of the Goddess must be ignored to make that point.

FOR FURTHER READING

Baring, Anne, and Cashford, Jules. *The Myth of the Goddess*. New York: Penguin, 1991. Print.

Eisler, Riane. *The Chalice and the Blade*. New York: Harper & Row, 1988. Print.

Gadon, Elinor W. *The Once and Future Goddess*. San Francisco: HarperSanFrancisco, 1989. Print.

Gimbutas, Marija. *The Language of the Goddess*. New York: Harper & Row, 1989. Print.

———. *The Goddesses and Gods of Old Europe*. Berkeley: University of California Press, 1982. Print.

Grant, Michael. *The Ancient Mediterranean*. New York: Meridian, 1988. Print.

Levy, Gertrude Rachel. *The Gate of Horn*. London: Faber & Faber, 1946. Print.

Marshack, Alexander. *The Roots of Civilization*. Kingston, RI: Moyer Bell Limited, 1991. Print.

Mellaart, James. *Catal Huyuk, A Neolithic Town in Anatolia*. New York: McGraw-Hill Book Co., 1967. Print.

Mohen, Jean-Pierre. *The World of Megaliths*. New York: Facts on File, Inc. 1990. Print.

Neumann, Erich. *The Great Mother.* Princeton, NJ: Princeton University Press, 1963. Print.

Sieveking, Ann. *The Cave Artists.* London: Thames and Hudson, 1979. Print.

Sjoo, Monica, and Mor, Barbara. *The Great Cosmic Mother.* New York: Harper & Row, 1987. Print.

Stern, Philip Van Doren. *Prehistoric Europe, From Stone Age Man to the Early Greeks.* New York: W.W. Norton & Co., 1969. Print.

Streep, Peg. *Sanctuaries of the Goddess, The Sacred Landscapes and Objects.* Boston: Bullfinch Press Book, 1994. Print.

Von Cles-Reden, Sibylle. *The Realm of the Great Goddess.* London: Thames and Hudson, 1961. Print.

CHAPTER 3

Mountain Mother

WHILE I WAS WANDERING THROUGH THE ISRAEL Museum in Jerusalem I spied a small metal statue from Ashod, dated from the 14 century BCE. It was a high backed chair, the type we associate with thrones, but this chair had a head and breasts. The noncommittal museum card accompanying it read "A woman and seat made as one." Later I saw a photograph of the same artifact, the caption this time read, "A Canaanite Goddess." Now tell me how does a chair get to be a deity or a deity get to be a chair? Of course when you think of the names of the parts of the chair they still keep the memory of the human body—arms, legs, and back; so I guess thinking of a chair as a human is really not so strange. But a woman/chair as a deity is still odd and worthy of some investigation.

In ancient days such a form represented the goddess as the mother who, by sitting, makes a lap for her child. Erich Neumann, in *The Great Mother*, tells us that Isis, the ancient Egyptian Mother Goddess, is the classic example of the Goddess being the seat. Her name means seat or throne and in front of the crown on her head is a chair. This imagery says the throne of the Pharaoh is the Goddess, and that the Pharaoh gets his power by sitting on the throne. In other words, symbolically he is sitting on the lap of the Great Goddess who is Egypt.

Ashdoda, the Canaanite Goddess in the form of a chair

Neumann tells us the person who sits on the throne is symbolically saying, "I am adopted by the Mother Goddess. Because I have been adopted by her I am reborn as her child. Now that I am the child of the Goddess I am immortal and divine." According to the ancients, once the ruler becomes one of the immortals, he now has the sacred power to rule the land. Remember in school we learned about the kings in history who ruled absolutely under the mandate of the "divine right of kings." This is where that idea comes from. I always wondered how the kings of old acquired their total control.

Today a throne is still an important symbol. Neumann points out our language describes this idea in such phrases as "ascend to the throne" and the "power of the throne." I must confess I never before thought of the throne this way. I always assumed the throne was important because the ruler sat in it. It never occurred to me that the ruler was important because he or she sat on the throne.

Through time, the connection of the throne to the female was blurred. My favorite illustration of this occurred in Israel while I was in a tour bus on the way to Bethlehem. The tour guide pointed out a tiny ancient church. He then said, "This is where Mary rested on her way to Bethlehem. In Jerusalem there are three other old churches where Mary rested. We call them Seats of Mary." At that, I perked up. To me a Seat of Mary is very different from a place where Mary rested. "Mary rested," has a nice passive quality describing a weary pregnant lady trudging her way to Bethlehem. The Seat of Mary rings of strength, like "seat of power," or "county seat" or "seat of wisdom." While the old imagery here remains, its power certainly is diminished.

According to Neumann, in the earliest days the original throne was the mountain. The mountain was one of the most common ways of expressing the presence of the deity. The ancients saw the mountain with its bulk, caves, and height as the body of the Great Goddess. It is a powerful presence which very visibly rules over the land. All the great mountains in ancient days were seen as the Goddess "sitting" on the earth. Many of the old names for the great peaks have feminine names. For example, Mt. Everest's original name meant "Goddess-Mother of the Universe." Nearby stands another peak called "Great Breasts full of Nourishment." When I was in Ireland I saw the double peaks called the "Paps of Anu." Anu was the Irish ancestral Goddess and paps refer to breasts. Twin peaked mountains throughout the world are tied to "nourishment" legends.

The throne also was used as the symbol of the presence of the Goddess. Frequently the ancients combined both the symbol of the throne and the mountain, like having a throne on the top of the mountain. In Macedonia, Greece, and Crete there are mountains which have on their summits huge thrones carved from rock. These are empty thrones waiting for the Goddess. It's hard to say from this imagery which piece is the mountain, which is the throne and which is the Goddess. They all get blended together like my metal statue of the goddess as a throne.

The ancient world thought the entire landscape of the earth itself was the body of the goddess. The mountains were her breasts and, if the mountains formed clefts, they were thought of as her *mons Veneris*, from which comes life. This expression is interesting because it means "Mount of Venus" which is both a mountain shrine and a reference to the female genitals. The caves were her womb; to enter them was to enter the Mother herself, a very serious and sacred trip. Most sacred, then, became the caves up on the high places.

For the ancients, part of the power of the mountains came not only by the bulk of the mountain representing the Goddess, but also because they thought the peaks of the mountains were a point of access to heaven. Mircea Eliade in *The History of Religious Ideas*, tells us such peaks were called cosmic mountains. He then tells us the top of a cosmic mountain was what the ancients called the center of the world. They felt the center of the world was the point where the three regions of heaven, earth and underworld met. This was the most sacred place possible in an ancient community.

Each ancient nation had its own center of the world and each thought its center of the world was the highest place in the world. Each nation then placed into their center its capital or chief temple. Theodore Gaster in *Myth, Legend and Custom in the Old Testament* says cities such as Nippur, Larsa and Sippar were so regarded and, of course, the best-known one is probably Jerusalem.

Many centers of the world were also called navels of the world. The center or navel of the world frequently was marked by a stone called an *omphalos*, Greek for navel or center of the world. For the ancient, to be at the navel of the world meant to be in the middle, the hub, the true world. This spot was important because at the navel of the world heaven, earth and the underworld were connected; from that intersection, they could communicate between the three regions. Throughout history, religious people have always felt the need to live as near as possible to what they considered to be the center of their world. Neumann gives us two examples of ancient shrines that are navels of the world. They are the Sanctuary at Delphi and the Temple of Jerusalem.

Delphi is the place of the famous Greek oracles. It is a breathtaking place and, although it sits high on the slopes of a mountain terrace, it is dwarfed by the even greater crags of Mt. Parnassos. An overpowering presence comes from the soaring heights, the scent of pines, coolness, and the darkness of the forest (very rare in that part of the world). The sacred spring of the sanctuary gushes out of the rock; and overhead a piece of intense blue sky is crossed with an occasional soaring bird. To get to Delphi, you climb and climb and climb, and arrive totally exhausted, and with a mind open to have an intense experience.

For more than a thousand years, Delphi was the spiritual center of the Hellenic culture. The shrine is the oldest religious sanctuary in Greece. Later in Greek history, Delphi became a Temple of Apollo. But before Apollo conquered Delphi when the Aryans conquered the Greeks, the site was a shrine to the Earth Mother. This we know from the legends and stories told of the shrine and from the name itself. The name Delphi is derived from *delphys*, "womb." Eliade tells us it takes its name from the mysterious cavity over which the Pythia (priestess) sat. The cavity was a mouth, a *stomion*, a word that meant vagina. Near the cavity stood the *omphalos*. It was the symbol of being the center of the earth. I saw a copy of the ancient *omphalos* in the museum at Delphi. Since I didn't know what an *omphalos* was, to me, with its marble carved in a rounded top, it looked more like a penis than a navel. Yet legend says it was a female symbol.

According to Greek legend, when the sanctuary was a Temple of Apollo, after the Pythia (priestess) washed in the water of the sacred fountain, she would seat herself on a bronze tripod over the deep chasm while she rested her hand on the *omphalos*. Fumes emerged from the chasm and the Pythia went into a trance. Some scholars think she drank a laurel-leaf brew to put herself in a trance. She then pronounced some sounds, which were translated by the priest. Today there are no traces of the chasm or its chamber. What happened to them is a great mystery. Some believe earthquakes eliminated them. The shrine itself was destroyed when Christianity overcame the power of Pagan Rome.

The other ancient center of the world mentioned by Neumann is Jerusalem. It has been a sacred site from at least the time of King David, which is 3,000 years ago. This is past the time of the Goddess culture and well into the Patriarchy. In the old city of Jerusalem stands the Temple Mount. While the Mount itself is not very high over the surrounding neighborhood, Jerusalem itself is quite high. Whenever we make the ascent to Jerusalem I am always surprised to realize my ears are popping.

According to the Hebrew scholar and anthropologist Raphael Patai in *Man and Temple*, it is the summit of Mt. Moriah on the Temple Mount which was the site of King Solomon's Temple, the most sacred spot on earth to the Israelites. Today the summit of Mt. Moriah is inside the Dome of the Rock. I found it very strange to see a mountaintop inside a building.

Patai describes how the site looked at the time of King Solomon's Temple. In the middle of the Temple, and acting as the floor of the Holy of Holies, was a huge native rock, which was part of the summit of Mt. Moriah. Jewish legends gave the rock the features of an *omphalos*, a navel of the earth. This rock, called in Hebrew, *Ebhen Shetiyyah*, the Stone of Foundation, was according to Jewish legends, the first solid thing created by God out of the primeval waters.

According to tradition, here is where Abraham built an altar and bound Isaac ("the land of Moriah," Genesis 23:2). The Jewish Temple built on Mt. Moriah was different from the synagogue, church or mosque of today. It was, as were all ancient temples, built not as a place where people congregated to worship but as a dwelling place on earth for God. Only priests were permitted to enter. While the imagery in Jewish tradition for this sacred site is male, the imagery of mountain and navel connect the site to an earlier female tradition. Today the Dome of the Rock is a Muslim monument, not a mosque, called *Haram al Sharif*. Mt. Moriah is sacred to Muslims because here is the place from which Muhammad ascended to heaven.

As Neumann reminds us, the thing to remember is that all ancient nations, in order to structure sacred space, had their own cosmic mountains and centers of the world. Some of these are still holy today. Many of the sites are on mountains, and in very ancient days humans thought of their most sacred symbols, mountains and thrones, as female.

Today few see the deity as an actual physical presence in the world around us, nor do many honor or feel awe by the sheer bulk and presence of the figure of the mother. Therefore the ideas expressed in these images rationally should have no hold on us. Yet writing this material, I was surprised to find that, as someone raised in the Jewish tradition, I was shocked at the idea of pairing the sacredness of Jerusalem with that of Delphi. Logically of course my feelings made no sense. Both are ancient, the legends and customs from the most ancient period of the one fit with the other.

The Temple Mount in Jerusalem today is still an active sacred site. The special aura of the ancient ideas of God living on the mountain surrounding Jerusalem even today is demonstrated by observant Jews who will not go up to the Temple Mount for fear they inadvertently will step into the area of the "Holy of the Holies" which, during the existence of the Temple, was where God dwelled. I once had a conversation with an observant young Jewish woman about the thickness of her stockings. I commented, since it was summer, her heavy cotton hose must be quite warm. Her reply was no, that when she was home in Jerusalem, she wore heavy wool hose. When I asked her why, she answered, "It feels like the right thing to do as Jerusalem is so very holy and sacred." The pull is still there.

With this in mind, it should come as no surprise to learn that many ancient countries identified themselves as living at the navel or the middle of the world. China called itself "The Middle Kingdom of Earth." Scandinavians called themselves "Midgard" or Middle-Earth. Old Japanese poems called Japan "The Middle Kingdom of Earth." Romans called the sea at the middle of its empire Mediterranean, which means Middle-of-the-Earth. Mexico means "navel of the moon."

To bring the imagery down to today, I love sitting in "thrones." Sitting in high-backed chairs makes me feel very special. The high-backed Oriental rattan ones are particularly nice. They make me feel like an empress. Also I love being in valleys surrounded by high mountains. It gives me a wonderful warm protected feeling. Artists still evoke reactions with this imagery. Among a group of pictures portraying ancient mother and throne images, I came across a picture of a sculpture called Madonna and Child, which Henry Moore did in 1945. It is a figure of a large, bulky seated mother, so large she looks like a big throne, whose arms are encircling the small child seated in her lap. The power of the relationship between the mother (the throne) and the child, even today, still works.

FOR FURTHER READING

"Archeological Romance." *Biblical Archaeological Review.* July–August 1993. Print.

Baring, Anne, and Cashford, Jules. *The Myth of the Goddess.* New York: Viking, 1991. Print.

Eliade, Mircea. *A History of Religious Ideas, Vol. I, From the Stone Age to the Eleusinian Mysteries.* Translated: W. Trask. Chicago: University of Chicago Press, 1978. Print.

——. *Images and Symbols: Studies in Religious Symbolism.* Translated: P. Mairet. London: Harvill Press, 1961. Print.

——. *The Sacred and the Profane: The Nature of Religion.* Translated from French: W. R. Trask. New York: Harvest/HBJ Publishers, 1957. Print.

Gaster, Theodore H. *Myth, Legend, and Custom in the Old Testament.* New York: Harper & Row, 1969. Print.

Goodrich, Norma Lorre. *The Priestesses.* New York: HarperCollins, 1989. Print.

James, E. O. *The Ancient Gods.* New York: G.P. Putnam, 1960. Print.

Lev, Martin. *The Traveler's Key to Jerusalem.* New York: Knopf, 1989. Print.

Neumann, Erich. *The Great Mother.* Princeton, NJ: Princeton University Press, 1963. Print.

Patai, Raphael. *Man and Temple.* Jersey City, NJ: Ktav Publishing House, 1947. Print.

Sjoo, Monica, and Mor, Barbara. *The Great Cosmic Mother.* New York: Harper & Row, 1987. Print.

Walker, Barbara G. *The Woman's Encyclopedia of Myths and Secrets.* New York: HarperCollins, 1983. Print.

CHAPTER 4

The Judgment of Paris

WE ALL KNOW THE STORY OF THE JUDGMENT OF PARIS. This is the old Greek legend in which Paris, the son of Priam of Troy, is called by Hermes, the messenger of the Gods, to judge a beauty contest among the three Goddesses—Aphrodite, Hera and Athene. The prize is a golden apple. All three goddesses try to bribe Paris, but Aphrodite tells Paris that, if she wins the golden apple, she will give him the beautiful Helen, wife of Menelaus of Sparta. Paris—surprise, surprise—of course gives the golden apple to Aphrodite. Paris then abducts Helen from her husband and so sets the stage for the Trojan War. Only one thing is wrong with the story. The symbols of the story tell a different tale, a tale that is much older than the story being told. Somewhere in time, from the era of the pre-Hellenic period to the story we know today, the story was twisted and the power focus shifted. Let's take a look at the symbols, starting with the three Goddesses and see if we can unearth the first story.

In the ancient world, Goddesses frequently were shown in threes. When they were, a very strong power form was being invoked. Such a grouping was called a Triple Goddess. Ancient artifacts and legends are full of such triads. According to Marija Gimbutas, in *The Language of the Goddess*, the traditional representation of the Triple Goddess is the Virgin-Mother-Crone, which comes from the three phases of the moon. These representations demonstrate the different functions of the Great Goddess as " life-giving, death-giving and transformational, rising, dying and self-renewing." As Gimbutas tells us, the symbolism of the Triple Goddess is based on the idea of eternal transformation in constant and rhythmic change from birth and destruction, birth and death.

From the beginning of civilization, three has been a very important number. Three was important because it expressed the idea of change. The earliest artifacts often have three parallel lines carved into them. Other symbols, such as fish, nets, zigzags or snakes, frequently accompany the three parallel lines. According to archeologist Gimbutas, all these symbols relate to the female deity, the Great Goddess. Triple-signs and triplicity are found in ancient tombs. When the symbols are in tombs, the triangles seem to symbolize the Goddess as owner of the triple source of the energy necessary for the renewal of life. Today, we still think of three as the magic number of transformation. Think of all the stories involving the number three, from Dorothy clicking the ruby slippers three times to get back to Kansas, to Jonah sitting in the whale three days to undergo a change of heart and mind, to Jesus being buried for three days before being resurrected.

The Jungian Erich Neumann, in *The Great Mother*, suggests that early humans used three not only because it demonstrated the changing phases of the Great Goddess, but also because, psychologically, three felt right. He says the earliest humans thought of themselves, without even being aware of it, as the center of the world. In that way, everything related to them. They then projected the image that came from their own unconscious onto the universe around them. The structure they created consisted of an image with a heaven above, the earth on which they and all living things live in the middle, and the underworld that is the dark space under them. In other words, the world was divided into the three parts of heaven, earth and underworld because, inside our heads and souls, that is the way we see and feel it. I remember, while in China some years ago, being shown an old theater with a stage in three layers so the action of the play could take place in any of the three worlds. Remember, Jungians believe inside every modern human remains a core of Stone Age (or older) beliefs and perceptions. Keeping that explanation in mind, a three-part division, with humans in the center, not only describes a changing pattern, but it still feels right.

Some of the oldest artifacts and wall carvings showing the Triple Goddess come from Catal Huyuk, a city from the seventh century BCE in what is now Turkey. From this site, we have clear images of the Triple Goddess in her standard form of a young maiden, a birth-giving matron, and an old woman or crone. These images represent the life cycle of a woman; and the popularity of the representation goes from pre-history, through history, down to time even beyond the rule of Rome. The three Goddesses together represented the deity as a dynamic, ever-changing cyclical power. The cycle goes from birth-to-life-to-death-and-then-to-birth again. These representations demonstrate the different functions of the Goddess. The cycle is ongoing and never stops. As you can see, the Triple Goddess figure is very powerful, not the sort of image one sees as being judged in a beauty contest. Instead, the Triple Goddess is more likely to be doing the judging rather than being judged; and she certainly is not likely to be part of a beauty contest. Gimbutas says that the concept of regeneration and renewal is perhaps the most outstanding and dramatic theme in this symbolism. The ancients thought of time in images of cycles. We moderns think of time as linear, with a beginning and an end. Each view creates a different world structure.

The Greek letter Delta is a triangle. It was a sign for woman showing her genital "Holy Door" of birth. Barbara Walker tells us that the name of the ancient Goddess Demeter refers to the Delta or triangle and then "meter," meaning mother. The ancients regarded each of the points of Demeter's triangle as being a different goddess, the three making one. This is the ancient idea of the Triple Goddess. One point was a Virgin, one a Mother and the third point the Crone.

Before we leave the Triple Goddess, let's take a further look at the Goddesses themselves. The first is Aphrodite, who was born from the sea. According to Robert Graves, in *The White Goddess*, sea images are usually related to the early pre-patriarchal period. Aphrodite is said to be older than time; she is the ancient mother of all on-going creation. She is a virgin in the original sense. This means She always belonged to herself and was independent. Since we know her as the Goddess of Desire, we know She had a close connection with sexuality. Every spring, her priestesses at Paphos bathed themselves and their idol in the sea, and all rose again, renewed. This is another way of saying they renewed their virginity, something that in the ancient world obviously meant something other than what we think of its being. The idea is probably closer to the cycle of the renewing vegetation in the spring than the concept of virginity common today. When Aphrodite was incorporated into the patriarchal Greek mythology, She was made into something far less powerful and far more frivolous than She had been in the matrilineal world.

Hera was the Mother of the Gods, who fed the gods the ambrosia of eternal life. According to Norma Goodrich in *Priestesses*, She is a most ancient Goddess, whose worship dates to before the coming of the Greeks. Graves tells us she is the pre-Hellenic Great goddess. Her forced marriage to Zeus portrays the conquests of Crete and Mycenae by the invading Greeks. In pre-Hellenic days, She had no consort. In order to control her, the patriarchal Greeks changed her to the quarrelsome wife of Zeus. She had been and still was the Queen of Heaven. She also remained the Goddess of women, their support and protectress in childbirth. Certainly she makes a fine mother figure. Hera was also the owner of the sacred apple tree in the far western paradise, which the Greeks called the Garden of the Hesperides. The West for the ancients was a place of death, like in sunset or moonset, while the East was a place of birth like in sunrise or moonrise. At Olympia, girl races were run in Hera's honor far before the 7th century BCE when the boys' races began.

Athene is also interesting. She originally was a Cretan Goddess who watched over the home and town. From her associations with trees and snakes, we know she originally was involved with fertility and renewal. When the patriarchal Greeks adopted her, they gave her a martial character and had her born from the head of her father Zeus. Barbara Walker, in *The Crone*, tells us that, in that role, she becomes the classic "wisdom" Goddess. Wisdom is one of the functions the ancients gave to the Crone, who was considered wise because she no longer shed the lunar "wise blood," but kept it within. The Crone is also shown in other forms that represented old age or death, or any of the other symbols of the dissolution that precedes regeneration. While the Crone was frequently shown as an old hag with long matted hair and big teeth, as a Wisdom Goddess she could be as beautiful as Athene. You can see then that the three goddesses in the so-called beauty contest are very much the manifestation of the Triple Goddess, the most powerful representation of the deity there could be.

The ancients used color symbolically, much as we do today. Ask anybody in Philadelphia during Eagles seasons when the city is plastered with green. Traditionally, the colors of the Triple Goddess are white, red, and black. White is the color for the virginal phase, red for the menstrual blood of the full moon phase, and black, the color of wisdom, which represents the Crone. Some writers also talk about black as the color of fertility, such as rich soil or the womb, while white is the color of bones and death. Either way, the three colors together symbolized the Triple Goddess. Walker tells us that, in India, these colors were known as the gunas or "strands," the interweaving threads of living nature. To the Romans, the three colors of red, white and black together always meant a religious ceremony or sacrifice. The same was true for the Celts, as is illustrated by the story of Percival, who fell into a trance because he saw a black bird and red blood on the white snow. Buried in a back room at the Museum of Archaeology and Anthropology of the University of Pennsylvania, the earliest Iranian artifacts are on display. There, I found a display of inlaid red, black and white colored ceramic cones from a wall in Sumer dating from the second half of the fourth millennium BCE. If you are counting, the wall is over five thousand years old. An accompanying photograph of the wall shows the cones were laid out in a decorative geometric pattern of the style those scholars who speculate about such things associate with the Goddess.

Ancient people saw magic everywhere, and with that, saw manifestations of their deity in all kinds of shapes, colors and/or numbers. It is no surprise, then, that the apple with its red skin, white fruit and black seeds always had a close connection to the Great Goddess. Stories of magic apples of death and/or immortality go through all Western literature. Remember, the Great Goddess not only deals with life but also death. Gimbutas tells us that the stories range from Hera feeding the Gods on apples from her western garden paradise, to King Arthur setting sail for Avalon ("the apple land of eternal life" in the West) accompanied by three fairies (the Triple Goddess again) to Snow White, whose wicked stepmother gave her a poisoned apple. The Scandinavians thought the apple was essential to resurrection and placed them in graves. Gimbutas tells us the Germans have a legend of the Winter Goddess, Frau Holla, who is an old hag. Along with other tasks, each spring, she is transformed into a frog and brings the red apple, symbol of life, back to earth from the well into which it fell at harvest. Roman banquets always went from eggs to apples, beginning with the symbol of creation and ending with the symbol of completion. Apples carried souls from one body to the next. The Yule pig was roasted with an apple in its mouth, which then served as a heart in the next life.

Apples also have an erotic connection. According to Theodore Gaster, in *Myth, Legend and Custom in the Old Testament*, throwing apples at a person was an invitation to dalliance. We bob for apples on Halloween because apples eaten then could show a young person his or her future spouse. Walker tells us that gypsy lovers sliced the apple across the core to reveal the sacred star or pentacle of the apple, and shared it before and after intercourse. They also ate the apple cut this way at weddings. Graves tells us that the pentacle at the core of the apple is the ancient emblem of immortality. It represents the Goddess in her five stations of life, from birth to death and back to birth again. The pentacle is also present in the natural five-pointed rose and the apple blossom. The Romans knew the rose as the Flower of Venus; and her prostitute-priestesses wore it as a badge of office. Apple blossoms are used as wedding flowers because they represent the virgin form of the Goddess, whose maturity produced the fruit.

Now let's get back to Paris and his story. It is easy to see the version we tell today makes no sense at all. When I expressed to my daughter the silliness of the idea that a mortal could judge a Goddess, she told me that my then six year old granddaughter returned from a story hour where this was the story. The child, quite annoyed, demanded that her mother explain how Athene, the Goddess of Wisdom, could get involved with anything as stupid as a beauty contest. Amazing, after 2,500 years of patriarchal nonsense, finally we are raising a generation who understands when something doesn't make sense.

So what is most likely the story under the story? Well, Joseph Campbell, in *Occidental Mythology*, suggests the presence of the Triple Goddess and their giving of the apple to Paris in all likelihood meant he was a candidate for a ritual sacrifice; or he could have been a god or hero receiving from the Triple Goddess the apple to mark his journey to death. The presence of Hermes in the story makes this interpretation even more sure, since Hermes was the God of Souls who traditionally transported the dead to the underworld. The story is not yet totally finished, as even Helen of Troy is not what she appears to be. She is no ordinary beautiful woman; she is the Spartan Moon Goddess who was also called Helle or Selene. You can very well ask what all this does to the story of Troy. Remember, the Greeks were the new patriarchal order while the Trojans were still under the old matrilineal rule. The fight was over the Bronze Age trade route through the Hellespont. This was a fight that the patriarchal Greeks won and, by doing so, they defeated and destroyed another community of the Great Goddess.

FOR FURTHER READING

Campbell, Joseph. *Occidental Mythology*. New York: Viking Press, 1964. Print.

———. *Creative Mythology*. New York: Viking Press, 1970. Print.

Gadon, Elinor W. *The Once and Future Goddess*. New York: HarperCollins, 1989. Print.

George, Demetra. *Mysteries of the Dark Moon*. San Francisco: HarperSanFrancisco, 1992. Print.

Gimbutas, Marija. *The Language of the Goddess*. New York: Harper & Row, 1989. Print.

Goodrich, Norma Lorre. *Priestesses*. New York: HarperCollins, 1989. Print.

Graves, Robert. *The Greek Myths, Vols. 1 & 2*. New York: Viking Penguin, 1955. Print.

———. *The White Goddess*. New York: HarperCollins, 1966. Print.

Neumann, Erich. *The Great Mother.* Princeton, NJ: Princeton University Press, 1963. Print.

Walker, Barbara. *The Crone.* San Francisco: HarperSanFrancisco, 1985. Print.

———. *Encyclopedia of Myths and Symbols.* New York: HarperCollins, 1983. Print.

———. *The Woman's Dictionary of Symbols and Sacred Objects.* New York: HarperCollins, 1988. Print.

CHAPTER 5

The Lady of the Moon

ONE OF THE SUMMER ACTIVITIES I MOST ENJOY IS SITting on a porch at the beach, watching a full moon rise in the sky while casting its silver reflection over the ocean. Who is not affected by this sight? In China and Japan, there were and still are special moon-watching parties just to watch the full moon. The moon, even in today's disconnected world, is still a source of delight and wonder. In ancient societies, the moon was this and much more.

Each 29.53 days, the moon completes one lunar orbit around the earth. As Evan Hadingham, in *Early Man and the Cosmos*, tells us, this circling of the earth is the same, month in and month out, year in and year out. Each month, the moon starts out as a sliver, swells to a full circle, diminishes to a sliver once more, finally disappears for three days, and then starts all over again. For us, this is a very ordinary event, yet for the ancients this ongoing cycling shaped the world and their beliefs. According to Demetra George, in *Mysteries of the Dark Moon*, as the ancients watched the moon changing its shape, place and color each night, it came to symbolize the cycle of transformation and the capacity for one thing to change into another. George tells us that women seemed to have this power of transformation since they were the ones who managed the daily mysteries.

For example, through cooking grain, grass became bread; and, of course, women also were able to transform their blood into milk to nourish babies.

As the great light shining in the darkness of the night, the moon, in all mythologies up to the Iron Age (c. 1250 BCE), was regarded as one of the supreme images of the Goddess. She was the measure of the cycle of time. She governed the menses of women, the waters of the sea and all the phases of increase and decrease. The seasons followed each other in sequence, as the phases of the moon followed each other. What was created was a cycle whose entirety could never be seen.

Not only was the moon itself significant, but each of its phases also had a special meaning. There were four phases in all, the three light phases of the lunar cycle, waxing, full and waning, and the fourth phase, the dark of the moon, which is the three days of darkness between the waning moon and the new moon. Sometimes the symbols of the moon refer to three phases; less commonly, they refer to four.

Esther Harding, in *Woman's Mysteries*, says that throughout all history both the new moon or crescent, as well as the waxing moon, have been considered good luck symbols, particularly in matters related to increase. They have been used to bring increase of flocks, herds, corn, and more especially, increase in the family. This was the time to plant, and to marry.

When I was in China, I was told the roof edges on buildings and bridges were curved like the crescent moon for luck. Even though the waning moon also creates a crescent, when the term crescent moon is used, it refers to the new moon. In the ancient traditions, during the waxing moon, all those things that need to grow had to be done. Planting took place during the first quarter of the moon, so the seed did not rot in the ground. Sheep were sheared under the waxing moon, so the wool would grow quickly again.

The time of the full moon was also important. In China, occasionally we saw a round "moon door," a good luck symbol. In the Jewish calendar, which is a lunar one, all the seasonal festivals start at the evening of the full moon. Harding tells us that an old common folk belief was that the light of the full moon made woman pregnant. To prevent this, women of many cultures were cautioned not to sleep in the light of the full moon. To this day, people believe strange things happen at the full moon.

Harding tells us that in most primitive communities, the women had charge of all matters concerned with food supply, except the hunting and killing of game. Planting, cultivating, and harvesting were all women's tasks in the ancient world. The ancients thought only women could make things grow. This is because they felt women must be of the same nature as the moon, not only because they could, as Harding puts it, "swell up" as the moon does, but also because of their monthly cycle which is of about the same length as the moon's. The word for menstruation and the word for moon are either the same or are closely related in many languages.

The waning moon, however, represented the powers of destruction and death. As George says, for any project which needed growth this was an unlucky time. However, it was a good time to do certain things, such as cutting trees so the wood aged well, or cutting grain so it didn't sprout. The waning moon also was the time for nature to be destructive. This was when floods, storms, disasters and pests were expected.

The trickiest phase of all was the dark of the moon. According to George, these three moonless days were a very scary time for the ancients in many lands. The dark phase of the cycle contained everything that they could not see with the waking eye, nor understand with the rational mind. All this made the dark of the moon a time of fear and awe. Many communities dealt with the disappearance of the moon by stopping all activity until the new moon appeared. According to Kathleen Cain in *Luna Myth & Mystery*, in most of the world, the dark of the moon is associated with death.

George tells us the dark of the moon symbolized divination, illumination and the powers of healing. Over the centuries, as people no longer worshiped the moon as goddess, the mysteries of the dark moon became associated with terror and evil. Because the dark of the moon is both the end of the cycle and the beginning of a new cycle, it makes transformation possible. This is because it contains the power either to destroy or to heal and regenerate. All cycles have a dark phase, a natural time that permits regeneration. When life is experienced as being linear, the dark time is the time of endings. However, when life is understood as cyclic, the ending phase is known as the transition to renewal.

On the fourth night, when the first sliver of the crescent moon was seen, the ancients felt the moon was reborn and new life was beginning. Therefore, it was necessary for the community to know exactly when the dangerous period of the dark moon ended and the lucky period of the waxing moon began. The arrival of the new moon was cause for celebration. Since the lunar cycle is 29 and a fraction days, not easy to track, the determination of the exact time of the new moon was a very important task, something the chief or priest did. In China, the royal astronomer sent out heralds to formally announce the new moon. Among Jews, the shofar, a ram's horn (which by nature is curved like a crescent moon) is sounded at the new moon. Also, at each new moon, Jews have a minor festival, Rosh Hodesh, which today, religious Jewish feminists celebrate as a special women's festival.

The phases of the moon frequently were equated to the life of the female. Imagine the new silvery moon crescent as the virgin, the full moon as mother, and the waning moon as the crone descending into the darkness of death, only to rise again. Crones were felt to be the wisest of mortals, because they permanently retained the "wise blood" of menstruation which let them use their wisdom for the benefit of the community. That certainly awards post-menopausal women a more powerful role than our modern society gives. Many of the traditions developed at that time are still honored today, such as believing crescent shapes like horseshoes are symbols of good luck or in the negative, changing the powerful and respected Crone of yesteryear into the feared and hated witch.

Women's menstrual cycles have always been connected to the moon. Their cycles are about 28 days, which is the approximate time of the monthly lunar cycle. Cain tells us in many cultures, old and new, the moon is held to be the cause of menstruation. Therefore the ancients assumed the moon was female, and a personification of the Great Goddess. Moreover, they felt since She was female, the Goddess should menstruate; and so She did. Harding tells us that in India, the Mother Goddess was thought to menstruate regularly. During these times, the statues of the Goddess were secluded and bloodstained cloths were displayed as evidence that She had Her period.

In the same way, Ishtar, the moon goddess of ancient Babylon, was thought to menstruate at the full moon. At the time of the full moon, the moon does not seem to be either increasing or decreasing, it seems to be resting. Harding tells us the Babylonians called this time sabattu, which means "Heart-rest," or "a day of rest for the heart." Since they felt this was the day of the Goddess's menstrual period, it became a "taboo" day with restrictions similar to those placed on menstruating women. Therefore, on this day, it was unlucky to do work, eat cooked food or travel. On the day of the moon's menstruation everyone in the community, not only the women, came under the "taboo."

Originally, the taboo was once a month, at the full moon. Later, some scholars believe the same taboo was placed on the new moon, another period when care had to be taken. These scholars suggest that, later, all the quarters of the moon—new, waxing, full and waning—became thought of as a transition time of the Goddess. Fear of disrupting these transition times made the seventh day of each lunar phase a time certain activities were forbidden. The custom for doing this was in existence thousands of years before the biblical God "rested" on the seventh day.

Women who live closely with each other tend to menstruate at the same time. Studies show that more women tend to start their menstrual cycles at the new moon or the full moon than at any other time of the month. Today, biologists refer to this phenomenon as the "Wellesley syndrome." In a tribal village, to have the women of the village all start their periods either at the new moon or full moon must have been not only a powerful scene but also a strong pull for tying moon and women together.

George tells us that a woman's menstrual blood was a major factor in her power. The ancients felt the moon was the source of women's menstrual blood. This is the "wise" blood that does not cause death. It contained also the life spirit and the creative power of the Great Mother. Monica Sjoo and Barbara Mor say, in *The Great Cosmic Mother*, that ancient women withdrew during their menstrual periods to meditate, fast, pray and communicate with the Great Mother. George tells us that menstruating women were considered a source of power and energy for themselves and their matriarchal community. The males held this event in awe. The women used it as a time for renewal and psychic development.

In later times, under the Patriarchy, the awe changed to fear. A series of restrictive taboos were instituted. In these, menstruating women were regarded as "unclean" and able to cause actual physical damage to the male. As late as the nineteenth century, Westerners report of tribal villages where men sometimes were so frightened of female menstrual blood they believed a single drop could kill them, the gaze of a menstruating woman could mean death, and the touch of her hands on their weapons could create great harm on the hunt. Among traditional Jews, the prohibition of women being with the men on the altar (Bimah) stems from these fears.

Harding tells us that the Moon Goddess is the mother of a son, whom she controls. When he grows up, he becomes her lover and then dies, only to be born again as her son. This son/lover is the beginning of what was later called the Vegetable God. The Moon Goddess belongs to a matriarchal system. She is her own mistress, a virgin, one-in-herself. The Moon Goddess is always represented as virgin, in spite of the fact she has many lovers and is the mother of many sons, or of one son, who dies only to be born again and again, year after year. "Virgin" means no more than an unmarried woman.

Scholars feel the Virgin Mary, by her representation and attributes, seems to be related to the ancient great mother moon goddess of Syria, who was called "Goddess of the Moon" and "Mother of God." Medieval paintings of the Virgin frequently show her not only with a baby but also standing or sitting on the moon. My favorite of these is a Gothic woodcut I saw in Padua. In it, Mary is sitting on the crescent moon as if it were a swing. Among the moon names the church fathers gave her are "Moon of the Church," "Our Moon," "The Spiritual Moon," and "The Perfect and Eternal Moon." Mary, though, has only the positive attributes of the Moon Goddess.

The Moon Goddess lived her life in phases, displaying the qualities of each phase in turn. According to Harding, in the bright moon phase she was good, kind, and beneficent. In the phase that corresponds to the time when the moon is dark, she is cruel, destructive, and evil. The worshipers of the Moon Goddess saw no problem in the deity being both light and dark, creation and destruction. They found unity in this duality.

While the Moon Goddess is the mother of all living things, the life-giver, She also is the destroyer. As Harding tells us, floods are her favorite tool of destruction. She is the cause of rain, storm and tide as well as flood. She creates all life on the earth, but then brings floods, which overwhelm the life She created. As a giver of rain she is quite inconsistent. Not only does She send rain in the spring when the young crops need it, She also has a penchant for sending storms in August when the rain can destroy the crops. For this reason, special rites were enacted to induce the goddess, to prevent the coming of these harvest storms.

The Goddesses of the Moon are many. All of them are aspects of the Great Goddess. Harding tells us that in Western Asia and in Asia Minor, the chief deity for many centuries was a Great Goddess called Magna Mater or Dea Syria. In other countries and at other times, she had different names. All of these different goddesses shared, more or less, the same life story, attributes, and characteristics, which did not vary greatly even though the name of the religion changed from place to place. The worship of this Magna Mater is exceedingly old; but as far back as we can trace history, we find evidences of a Great Goddess who reigned supreme with her son, who usually is also her lover.

Harding also tells us that Ishtar of Babylon, who was also a Moon Goddess, is one of the oldest of the individual Great Mother goddesses. Before the Sumerians migrated to that part of the world, She was worshipped by the native populations. Before the Canaanites, Hebrews, and Phoenicians arrived at their corner of the Eastern Mediterranean, the native people of that area worshipped the mother goddess in the form of Astarte or Ashtart. Isis was worshipped in Egypt where she was called Mother of the Universe and Giver of all Life on Earth. Cybele, Goddess of Earth and Goddess of the Moon, was worshipped in Phrygia. In Western Europe as far west as Ireland, the deity from prehistoric times who was also the Celtic mother goddess was called Anu or Annis. Other names for her were "Goddess of Earth" and "Goddess of the Moon."

According to Harding, in the Babylonian account of the great flood, Ishtar, the Moon Goddess, causes the great flood but then saves from Her flood a remnant of Her people. Here the dual character of both life-giver and destroyer of the Moon Goddess is clear. The Old Testament story of the flood probably is derived from this more ancient tale of Babylonia. The same story is told in the tradition of China. There the Chinese Moon Goddess repeopled the earth by giving birth to all living things.

Over many thousands of years, the idea of the moon goddess changed with the cultures. Cain tells us in the earliest days of Greece, the moon goddess was one goddess named Selene. Later She was replaced by two distinct goddesses, Aphrodite the Bright Moon, and Hecate, the Dark Moon. In still later times, the Moon Goddess was sometimes called Hecate-the-Three-Headed, which was a combined form of the moon goddesses—Artemis, Selene and Hecate. This form demonstrated the moon's three phases. Artemis, the goddess of untamed nature was the crescent or waxing moon. Selene, who pulled the full moon across the sky with her chariot, was the full moon. Hecate, the goddess of the waning and dark moon, was the most powerful. She derived her power not only from her role as the destroyer, but also as the one who took the souls of the dead through the dark spaces of nonbeing to prepare them for being again. Newborn children and animals were sacrificed to her. Harding tells us She was the giver of rain, as well as harvest storms. Her major festival on August 13 was held in order to avert those storms. This festival was continued by the Catholic church when the date of August 15 was chosen as the celebration of the feast of the Assumption of the Blessed Virgin.

Marija Gimbutas, in *The Language of the Goddess*, says "the moon's phases—new, waxing, old—are repeated in several trinities that reflect these phases. There is maiden, matron, crone: life-giving, death-giving and transformational; rising, dying and self-renewing. Life-givers are also death-wielders. Immortality is created by the innate forces of regeneration within Nature." One way or another power of the moon is still there.

FOR FURTHER READING

Baring, Anne, and Cashford, Jules. *The Myth of the Goddess*. New York: Penguin, 1991. Print.

Cain, Kathleen. *Luna, Myth & Mystery*. Boulder, CO: Johnson Publishing Co., 1991. Print.

Eliade, Mircea. *Images and Symbols: Studies in Religious Symbolism*. Translated: P. Mairet. London: Harvill Press, 1961. Print.

George, Demetra. *Mysteries of the Dark Moon*. San Francisco: HarperSanFrancisco, 1992. Print.

Gimbutas, Marija. *The Language of the Goddess*. New York: Harper & Row, 1989. Print.

Grahn, Judy. *Blood, Bread & Roses: How Menstruation Created the World*. Boston: Beacon Press, 1993. Print.

Hadingham, Evan. *Early Man and the Cosmos*. New York: Walker Publishing Company, 1984. Print.

Hall, Nor. *The Moon & the Virgin, Reflections on the Archetypal Feminine*. New York: HarperPerennial, 1994. Print.

Harding, M. Esther. *Woman's Mysteries, Ancient & Modern*. Boston: Shambhala, 1990. Print.

Jung, C. G. *Collected Works, Vol. V: Symbols of Transformation*. Editors and Translators: G. Adler and R.F.C. Hull. Princeton, NJ: Princeton University Press, 1967. Print.

Neumann, Erich. *The Great Mother*. Princeton, NJ: Princeton University Press, 1963. Print.

Patai, Raphael. *The Hebrew Goddess*. Detroit, MI: Wayne State University Press, 1990. Print.

Sjoo, Monica, and Mor, Barbara. *The Great Cosmic Mother*. New York: Harper & Row, 1987. Print.

Spretnak, Charlene. *Lost Goddesses of Early Greece, A Collection of Pre-Hellenic Myths*. Boston: Beacon Press, 1981. Print.

Walker, Barbara. *The Crone*. San Francisco: HarperSanFrancisco, 1985. Print.
———. *The Woman's Dictionary of Symbols & Sacred Objects*. San Francisco: HarperSanFrancisco, 1988. Print.

CHAPTER 6

The Dark Goddess

SOMETIME AGO, DURING A VISIT TO SPAIN, A FRIEND went to the pilgrimage site of the Shrine of Our Lady of Montserrat, high in the mountains near Barcelona. The fourteenth century Benedictine Monastery there is where the monks worship Catalonia's Patron Saint, the Black Madonna of Montserrat, one of the most famous of the Black Madonnas. My friend found the experience very moving; so on returning home, she asked me what I knew about Black Madonnas. Not knowing anything, but thinking it couldn't be a big project, I said I would search the reference materials. Many, many pages of notes later, this is what I learned.

According to Esther Harding, in *Woman's Mysteries, Ancient & Modern*, there are in Europe, certain shrines of Mary, Mother of God, Moon of the Church, in which the image of Mary is black. These shrines are still major pilgrimage sites visited by pilgrims from far and wide. When I went to visit the Lady of Montserrat, there was a two-hour wait to see her. Not only was the line long, but the people (who did not seem to be tourists) were singing and praying when they reached the statue. This was a very serious event. The Black Virgin or Black Madonna figures are felt to have special powers for healing, for peace, for reaching the people directly; and some shrines are even places where miracles can occur.

Statues of Black Madonnas are often found in crypts or wells on the worship sites of the ancient goddesses. Some of the most famous cathedrals of Europe are sites containing Black Madonnas. In the cathedral of Chartres outside Paris there are two portrayals, one gazing out of a stained glass window, another in the crypt. Today, there is ever increasing interest in these images. As Demetra George, in *Mysteries of the Dark Moon*, says, these figures of very long ago, historically, were called the Dark Goddess, dating from a time when the moon was worshipped as a primary feminine divinity. The Dark Goddess was only one aspect of the Triple Goddess of the moon, who in those days ruled over the entire world. But it is the Dark Goddess who most resembles our Black Virgins. Anne Baring and Jules Cashford, in the *The Myth of the Goddess*, tell us black is the color associated with Wisdom, as the dark phase of the lunar cycle.

The Dark Goddess is known by many names in different lands. According to George, She is called Kali in India, Hekate and Persephone in Greece, Lilith in the Near East, Morgan in Britain, the Fates, the Furies, Medusa, Medea. The Gorgons, the Sirens, the Black Madonna, Black Isis, are some of Her other names. According to Begg, many of them are clus-

The Black Madonna of Montserrat

Kali

tered in the areas of Europe where worship of the ancient pagan goddesses lingered or where the Cathars flourished. Quite often there is a cult of Mary Magdalene and a Black Virgin in the same place. The cult of the Black Virgin seems to have links to hidden, dark secrets of the past.

As Caitlin Matthews, in *Sophia: Goddess of Wisdom*, says, the Black Goddesses were also known as Wisdom Goddesses. She lies at the basis of spiritual knowledge. She holds the treasures of the Divine Feminine, which lie deep within us, waiting to be discovered. This means not only the wisdom of things as they are, but wisdom of things as they always have been. I have read much material trying to establish a specific definition of what is meant by "Wisdom." The definitions are never clear. They are always shrouded by the language of whoever is expressing the concept, whether it be a mystical, religious, or spiritual definition. One way of stating it, if it helps, is that Wisdom deals with matters of the soul, those feelings and fears which really control our lives and which usually lie buried within us, but of which we may not even be aware. As Matthews says, "We feel at home with Wisdom because she has seen and heard it all before." Or as Anne Baring and Jules Cashford state it, "The foundation of Wisdom is the idea that the earthly, visible order of creation participates in the invisible source of being. In the ancient world the deity who controlled creation was also considered to be the deity in charge of All."

The Black Virgins are special, and there are a lot of them around, over 450 shrines in Europe alone. All the shrines of the Black Virgin have local legends to explain the blackness of the Madonna statues. While the legends differ from place to place, the most common explanation offered by the Church is that the images were probably charred in a fire or blackened through candle smoke or exposure to the elements. The problem with that explanation is that only the faces and hands of the Madonna and Child are black; their painted clothing is still colored. Regardless of the Catholic Church's explanation for the blackness of the Black Madonnas or Black Virgins, all seem to have links to the hidden and mysterious beliefs from thousands of years ago, in a time before recorded history.

Others offer different explanations. Followers of the psychologist Carl Jung see the blackness as a reference to the psychological dark side, which according to them is within each of us. Monica Sjoo and Barbara Mor, in *The Great Cosmic Mother*, suggest the blackness is a possible link to the blackness of the ancient goddesses of Egypt and Africa, whose worship spread from Africa to much of the rest of the world. Or perhaps, as Elinor Gadon in *The Once and Future Goddess* suggests, the Madonna is black because she is the Earth Goddess and the blackest earth is the richest and the most fertile. Or maybe she is black because, like the Hindu Goddess Kali, she represents the dark, the night, and death, and all those other aspects that the Western world has repressed through its fear of women, of female sexuality, and of dying. This, of course makes the ancient Hindu belief not far from the modern Jungian one.

Whatever the Black Virgin symbolizes, judging from her miracles, according to Kathleen Cain in *Luna, Myth & Mystery*, fertility and the home are Her major concerns. She also is often associated with esoteric teaching and schools of initiation. Powers of life and death over newborn babies are attributed to many Black Virgins. Black Virgins, wherever they are, seem to be favored for weddings, for help for childlessness, for illness.

Of all the ancient goddesses, three most likely were the model of the modern Black Virgin. These three not only were the most popular of the ancient goddesses, but they also were sometimes represented as black. They were Artemis, Isis and Cybele.

Let's first take a look at Artemis. I always think of Her, as well as Her Roman counterpart, Diana, as the Goddess of the Hunt—running through the forests accompanied by all the animals. However, She also was the ruler of women in childbirth, the mother of mountains, as well as the protector of animals. Of all the Greek goddesses, She was the one who received the bloodiest sacrifices. According to Baring and Cashford, Her name is not Greek; and there have been found inscriptions of Her name, which link Her with the old Minoan goddess of Crete. Begg tells us that according to legend, She started as a black meteoric stone discovered in a swamp by Amazons. Such a stone, known in French as *betyle*, from the Greek *baitulos*, both manifests the divine presence and signifies Bethel, the house of God. It is probable that the Phoenicians brought Her to Gaul with them in 600 BCE when they founded the city now called Marseilles. It is striking that the greatest numbers of Black Virgins occurs in areas where the Phoenicians had either settlements or important trading partners. Her shrine at Ephesus, which was one of the seven wonders of the ancient world, was built in a period from 334 BCE and finished in 250 BCE. The immense Roman alabaster and bronze statue in the shrine was built in the second century. It showed the Goddess with black face, hands and feet, many breasts, a small shrine on her head, and images of different animals on her dress. According to Baring and Cashford, She was a figure much beloved by the people of Ephesus; and it was when Her cult was repressed in 380 CE by the Church that the people of Ephesus turned to Mary. Tradition says that the Virgin Mary spent her final years at Ephesus; and according to Begg, it was in Ephesus in 431 AD that the Virgin Mary was proclaimed "Mother of God."

Begg tells us that by the beginning of the Christian era, the official Roman state religions no longer attracted the people. For a while, it seemed as if the dominant deity of the Roman Empire might again become the Great Goddess. It was during this period that the Goddesses Cybele and Isis were the most popular. Cybele, who is less familiar to us than other goddesses, is an ancient goddess who originally came from Anatolia (Turkey). According to Begg, Her history goes back to the New

Diana of Ephesus

Stone Age about 7,000 years ago to the Neolithic matriarchal civilization of Catal Huyuk. She was first worshipped as a black stone, probably a meteorite, and it was in this form that She came to Rome in 205 BCE, at the request of the Senate, since a prophecy in the Sibylline Books stated that only She could save Rome from Hannibal of Carthage. To the Romans, She was simply "Magna Mater," which means Great Mother. In Rome, Her main temple, which was built in 191 BCE, stood on the Palatine Hill where the Vatican now stands.

Like all the Great Goddesses who ruled over creation, She was guardian of the dead and the goddess of rebirth and wild life. She was not only popular in Rome, but Her cults were also active in Spain and France. Begg tells us Cybele became the supreme deity of Lyons, France, where a Black Virgin cult still flourishes today. A huge temple honoring Her once stood in Lyons; today, standing at that site is the great basilica of Notre-Dame de Fourvière and the Oratory (a structure other than a parish church used for prayer and the celebration of mass) of the Black Virgins. While Her lion is still on the arms of the city of Lyons, little else remains. Other examples of Black Madonna sites in areas where Cybele was popular are Aix-en-Provence and Madrid. It was in Madrid at the enormous fountain at the Plaza de Cibeles where I was amazed to encounter a huge statue of Cybele riding in Her chariot.

As with Artemis and Cybele, Isis's story was associated with life, death, and resurrection. Frequently, the Egyptian Goddess Isis' statues are black and show Isis with the child Horus in Her lap. The Black Madonna image my friend and I saw at Montserrat looks like a traditional statute of Isis with child. In Europe the center of the ancient Isis cult was Paris (*Par-isis*, the grove of Isis), and in Roman times the temple of Isis was at the western limit of the city. Today, on that site stands the famous abbey and church of Saint-Germain-des-Prés and Saint-Sulpice. There was a black statuette of the goddess at Saint-Germain-des-Prés that was honored as the Virgin until 1514, when it was destroyed. Begg tells us that the Benedictines of Saint-Germain, like the priests of Isis, are "wearers of the black," which is the traditional color of Wisdom.

The Goddess Isis had two aspects. She was the creator, mother, nurse of all, and also, as were many of the Dark Goddesses, She was the Destroyer who spread disease, war and death. In our world today we have no place to honor these negatives of human life. Harding tells us that Her name, Isis, means ancient. Matthews tell us She was a potent Goddess as early as the 3rd millennium BCE. She was also called Maat, which means Knowledge or Wisdom, a term which refers to the ancient wisdom. Matthews says that by about the 380's, Christianity had established itself as the Roman state religion. Pockets of paganism survived where the Goddess was still worshipped; but, all in all, the cult of the pagan deities was effectively outlawed. Devotion to the Blessed Virgin Mary replaced cults of the Goddess. However, until the fifth century, there is little evidence within the Church of goddess survival in the form of a Mary cult. Baring and Cashford tell us that, since the Goddess was very popular and the people would not renounce her, the Church eventually rededicated most of the Goddess sites, and transferred Her powers to the Virgin Mary. This took place sometime between 400 CE and 500 CE; and, according to Begg, this was particularly true with the Black Virgins. It took less than a century for Mary to take over the role of Isis, Cybele and Diana. The minor goddesses cults either just dwindled or were suppressed. Baring and Cashford say, "It appears as if the imagery of the older goddesses passed directly on to the figure of Mary, inspired by the needs of the people and perhaps also by the understanding of the priests that these long-established customs of devotion had to be understood in terms of the new religions. Isis and Cybele had been 'Mother of the Gods'; Mary was now 'Mother of God.'"

Baring and Cashford tell us that from the tenth century onwards, all through Europe, there was great interest in the Black Madonnas/Black Virgins. No one really knows why this period of time created an upsurge of popular devotion to the Virgin Mary, or why there was dramatic eruption of the feminine archetype in this period. The places sacred to Her began to draw huge numbers of devotees. The cult of the Black Virgin, according to Begg, is essentially a product of the 12th century Gothic renaissance. All kinds of pilgrims flocked to worship before the Black Virgin, seeking her favor and leaving great wealth at her shrines. Miraculous cures took place there. The people worshipped Mary as they had always worshipped the goddess. But the discomfort of the Catholic Church with the Black Madonna is quite understandable. Traditionally, She is associated with all kinds of awkward subjects that the Church had rejected and would prefer to ignore, such as the pre-Christian origins of much in Christianity, the Gnostics, the history of the Knights Templars, Catharism, the Cult of the Holy Grail, and the Church of Mary Magdalene.

Gadon says the Gnostics are dualistic, believing that spirit and matter are separate and that spiritual liberation comes from knowledge. The Cathars, a Gnostic sect allied with the Troubadours and their Courts of Love, were active in the south of France during the thirteenth century. They may have practiced ritual sex. Women were admitted to their priesthood and they were so threatening that the Papacy launched a successful Crusade against them. The Templars, a Crusading Order, learned about the mystery of the female divine in the East; and, on their return, actively promoted the cult of the Virgin. They were accused by the Inquisition of denying the validity of the sacraments, as well as other unspeakable heresies like sodomy, and were outlawed at the Council of Vienna in 1318. The cult of Mary Magdalene, which worships the Black Virgin, absorbed many of the esoteric teachings. According to the Gnostic Gospels, early Christian material was full of female motifs that were excluded from the official canon. Mary Magdalene was one of the original disciples of Jesus. Magdalene's cult is based on the legendary account of her settling in the area of Marseille after Jesus' death, where it was believed that she gave birth to Jesus' child. The cult of Mary Magdalene is linked to the Black Virgin because both continued to hold the female principle as sacred and divine.

As Gadon tells us, if we look into what Christianity has labeled heresy, we find within a different attitude toward the power of women and female sexuality. Heresy is often the inner truth of a way, which is other than that of the dominant view. According to her, "the traditional Christian notion of female sexuality is life denying, the heretical life affirming." These opposing views of the human condition create two different worldviews. Today, the Goddess is reemerging through the power of the women's movement, which is forcing us to reexamine our feelings about the roles and power of women.

Two Black Virgins, Guadalupe of Mexico and Our Lady of Czestochowa in Poland, are national symbols. The story of Guadalupe in Mexico is that the Virgin Mary appeared to Juan Diego, a humble Indian convert, and spoke to him in his Indian language. She commanded him to seek out the Archbishop of Mexico and inform him of her desire to see a church built in her honor on Tepeyac Hill. When the archbishop demanded some proof of the vision's authenticity, the Virgin wrought a miracle of making roses bloom in the arid desert. She told Diego to gather the flowers into his cloak and present the cloak to the archbishop. When he unfolded the cloak, the image of the Virgin was miraculously stamped on it. The shrine, which has been rebuilt several times in order to accommodate the increasing crowds of devotees, is today a basilica. To me, the most interesting thing about this story is that this was not the first religious structure built on Tepeyac. In pre-Hispanic times there was a temple located here to the Earth Goddess Tonantzin, which means Our Mother, who, like Guadalupe, was associated with the moon and was the center of a pilgrimage cult. Some Mexican Indians to this day continue to refer to the Virgin by her Indian name. The Virgin appeared at the site of Tonantzin's shrine only ten years after the Spanish Conquest, which not only was a military defeat but was also the defeat of the people's old gods and old ritual.

Poland is another country whose people, oppressed by centuries of foreign occupation, rallied under the patronage of a painting of the Black Madonna, Our Lady of Czestochowa. Since 1656 She has been honored as the "Queen of Poland," the symbol of national survival and religious liberty. Her history is a long one and Her miracles seem to be public ones. Legend says the painting was created by St. Luke, the evangelist. St. Helena, the Queen Mother of Emperor Constantine, found the portrait during her visit to the Holy Land and brought it to Constantinople in the fourth century. During her stay in Constantinople, She is reported to have frightened the besieging Saracens away from the city. Eventually, through the transfer of royal dowries, the painting made its way to Poland in the fifteenth century. In 1655, a small group of Polish defenders, with Her help, were able to drive off a much larger army of Swedish invaders. This was the event for which She is honored as the "Queen of Poland." Later on September 15, 1920, She dispersed an army of Russian invaders by appearing at the River Vistula. During its outlawed period, Solidarity, the revolutionary labor movement of Poland, chose Her as a symbol. Members who were afraid to wear insignia which identified them as part of the movement, wore buttons instead with the icon of the Virgin. When Solidarity leader Lech Walesa received the Nobel Peace Prize, he took the award medal to Her shrine for safekeeping.

Today, the Black Virgin is becoming even more popular. Begg tells us She was always helpful in easing the rigidity of the patriarchal rules. Traditionally, She is on the side of the people's needs whatever that might be. Politically, She is in favor of freedom, justice, and integrity, and for the rights of peoples, cities and nations to be independent from outside interference. Now that the patriarchal values are becoming less dominant and women are more able to become the force tradition says they were, Her message becomes even more important, as it provides a way for those, both men as well as women, searching for meaning and significance in their lives and relationships today.

The ancients saw the Goddess as a giver of life, and of all that promotes fertility as well as being the wielder of the destructive powers of nature. As Harding tells us, this was not a problem in the ancient world because the ancients saw the deity as ruling over all creation, both good and evil. In our world the deity is only good. As a result, today nearly all of the Great Mother's dark, fearsome, and devouring qualities have been removed from the Virgin. The Virgin is kind, gentle and forgiving. The closest she gets to anger is sorrow. Her dark side now exists primarily in the figures of the Black Virgins. But the power and with it the darkness of the ancient goddesses which came from negative energy, destruction, anger, and death find no place in our world today. This is, of course, a pity—because now we have no place to anchor and deal with these feelings and needs.

As Ean Begg says, "The ancient, battered, much-loved, little understood Black Madonnas are a still-living archetypal image that lies at the heart of our civilization. Her message of the strength of the Black Madonna is clear for us. The feminine principle is not a theory but in reality has a will of its own which we ignore at our peril. It cannot be controlled by others and cannot be forced against its will to go anywhere or do anything without serious consequences to those who try."

I feel her presence is important to help moderate our authoritative and patriarchal world. I learned a great lesson in Montserrat. I remember the awe and excitement I felt when I first saw the Lady of Montserrat in the church high above the figure of Jesus at the altar. I got weak in the knees, although religious events do not usually affect me strongly. But for me, the idea that an icon in the form of my sex was the power figure in this place was very exhilarating, empowering and hopeful.

FOR FURTHER READING

Baring, Anne, and Cashford, Jules. *The Myth of the Goddess*. New York: Penguin, 1991. Print.

Begg, Ean. *The Cult of the Black Virgin*. London: Arkana/Penguin Books, 1996. Print.

Cain, Kathleen. *Luna, Myth & Mystery*. Boulder, CO: Johnson Publishing Co., 1991. Print.

Carroll, Michael P. *The Cult of the Virgin Mary*. Princeton, NJ: Princeton University Press, 1992. Print.

Gadon, Elinor W. *The Once and Future Goddess*. New York: HarperCollins, 1989. Print.

George, Demetra. *Mysteries of the Dark Moon*. San Francisco: HarperSanFrancisco, 1992. Print.

Getty, Adele. *Goddess, Mother of Living Nature*. New York: Thames and Hudson, 1990. Print.

Harding, M. Esther. *Woman's Mysteries, Ancient & Modern*. Boston: Shambala, 1990. Print.

Matthews, Caitlin. *Sophia: Goddess of Wisdom*. New York: Thorsons, 1991. Print.

Osmen, Sarah Ann. *Sacred Places, A Journey into the Holiest Lands*. New York: St. Martin's Press, 1990. Print.

Sjoo, Monica, and Mor, Barbara. *The Great Cosmic Mother*. New York: Harper & Row, 1987. Print.

Walker, Barbara. *The Crone*. San Francisco: HarperSanFrancisco, 1985. Print.

———. *The Woman's Dictionary of Symbols & Sacred Objects*. San Francisco: HarperSanFrancisco, 1988. Print.

———. *The Woman's Encyclopedia of Myths and Secrets*. San Francisco: HarperSanFrancisco, 1983. Print.

CHAPTER 7

Making the World Go Round

To the ancients, sex and its symbols were a way to express cosmic concepts. In that world, both sex and sexual symbolism had a much broader meaning than they do to us moderns. In ancient days, sex was an important religious motif. According to Riane Eisler in *Sacred Pleasure*, the concept that sex has a spiritual dimension is very foreign to us. But the ancient art, legends and traditions very vividly tell us this was so for them. The ancients saw the female body and its parts and symbols as standing for the major cosmic ideas of birth, death, initiation and regeneration. Eisler tells us this sexual imagery is used constantly not only in ancient art but also in the classical work which followed. Because it is not part of our culture we are uncomfortable; it makes us moderns squirm. That's because the imagery means different things to us than to the ancients; to us, the naked female body and its parts and symbols are associated only with sexual arousal.

According to Barbara Walker in *The Woman's Dictionary of Symbols and Sacred Objects*, the holiest symbols of Paleolithic (Old Stone Age) and Neolithic (New Stone Age) humanity were the symbols of the womb, the source of life. Joseph Campbell tells us the Sanskrit word for a temple meant "womb." The Sumerian word for the underworld, the sacred cave, and the womb was *matu*, from the universal root word for "mother." The most revered oracle shrine in Greece was named Delphi, meaning "womb." All over the world, initiatory, baptismal, and consecration ceremonies use womb imitations to represent rebirth into a new condition of life. Yet today, we have lost this traditional imagery as well as the ability to understand it.

In *Civilization of the Goddess*, Marija Gimbutas tells us, that in the religion of Old Europe, death and regeneration are expressed as two interdependent but contiguous aspects of one deity. Although we moderns see death and birth as opposite ends in our linear thinking, the Great Goddess of the Stone Age holds both death and birth as part of the unbroken ever-repeating circular cycle. These communities regarded the Earth to be the body of the Goddess. We see a leftover from this idea in Genesis 2:7 where man is formed from earth. The word-form for earth used here is feminine. The form they used in the world of the Goddess to express this idea was the female vulva. Eisler tells us the vulva was a major symbol of birth, death, and regeneration. It was the magical door of life. Since the earth was feminine, all entrances into the earth were thought of as vulvas. This included such things as passages to caves, rivers, springs and wells, anything that went underground. Not only was it believed that all life came from here, as Monica Sjoo and Barbara Mor in *The Great Cosmic Mother* tell us, but when the dead were buried, the ancients believed they were returning to the womb of the Goddess for rebirth. Remember, to the ancients, earth is the body of the Goddess. The vulva was the symbol that demonstrated the life force and energy of the Earth.

The vulva's magic also included magical powers of spiritual illumination and transformation. Many common shapes were symbols for the vulva. One of the oldest, which was also the basic symbol of the Goddess, was the triangle. Barbara Walker, in *The Woman's Encyclopedia of Myths and Secrets*, says the delta, or triangle, in the Greek sacred alphabet, stood for the

Holy Door, vulva of the All-Mother Demeter ("Mother Delta"). In Egypt, the triangle was the hieroglyphic sign for "woman." Most ancient symbol systems used the triangle to stand for the Goddess's genital "holy place," source of all life. Some years ago on a back street of a village around Lake Como, Italy, I found some graffiti on a wall that used the triangle in exactly that way to express the idea of a vulva. But since this was a modern expression, the idea was "sexy," not reverential.

Because it was the common symbol for the vulva, Walker calls the horseshoe shape one of the most sacred in the ancient world. The difficulty that moderns have with these symbols for the vulva was clearly illustrated for me during an art lecture some years ago. I listened to the instructor blur the very point he was trying to make when he became entangled with the sexual symbols of ancient regeneration imagery and he left out the central symbolism of the painting he was discussing.

The painting was "The Oxbow," a large and powerful painting by Thomas Cole, which hangs in the Metropolitan Museum. According to the Metropolitan, Cole painted it in 1836, seeking the look of a landscape after a thunderstorm. In the painting the viewer looks down on the scene as if from a hill. On the left there are dark clouds and fallen trees and on the right, sunny skies and growing fields. In the middle, the section of the Connecticut River called the Oxbow, bends into the oxbow shape for which it is named. To my urban eyes, unfamiliar with oxbows, the bend looks exactly like a horseshoe. The lecturer focused on death and regeneration symbols in the painting. He went into great detail about the storm and death symbols on one side and the sun and growth symbols on the other. However, not once did he mention the horseshoe-shaped bend of the river, the painting's most prominent regeneration symbol—the oxbow shaped like a horseshoe. I don't know whether he was unaware that the horseshoe shape was an ancient symbol of regeneration standing for a woman's vulva, or whether he was

"The Oxbow" by Thomas Cole

reluctant to discuss so sexy an idea with a group primarily of women past middle age. But I do know that in this lecture, he certainly missed the major and central symbol of his argument.

The point he missed was that the goddess symbol for death and regeneration was the focal point of the painting. In the ancient world, the horseshoe was one of the most sacred symbols, not only because it marked entrances and exits, but especially because it marked those of major changes. The horseshoe shape, basically, is the same as the letter omega, the last letter of the Greek alphabet. Its position at the end of the alphabet makes it the symbol to mark all ends. As such, it stands for the side of the Goddess which deals with death. Today we still hang horseshoes "for luck" over doorways. In pagan days, this was done to protect the threshold.

Yet another expression of the vulva is the yoni, a double pointed oval in the shape of the external female genitalia. Its basic design is made by overlapping the edges of two circles of the same size in such a way that the edge of one goes through the center of the other. This shape frequently shows up on the floors of medieval cathedrals as a form of geometric decoration. Walker says, as the ancient seat of female sexual power, this symbol is still worshipped today by the Tantric Hindus of India. She tells us that Tantric Hindus regard female sexual power as the source of all creative action. They feel the energizing principle of the universe is the female orgasm. Personifying this energy is the Goddess Kali, who has the title of Cunti or Kunda, from which, of course, comes the root of the now obscene word "cunt" and all its relatives.

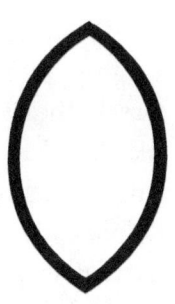

Today, we consider the word "cunt" to be so obscene that it is still excluded from serious dictionaries. Yet according to Michael Dame in *The Silbury Treasure: The Great Goddess Rediscovered*, the word is not slang, dialect or any marginal form, but has deep roots in language and is a word of the oldest stock. Many of its derivatives are not only standard words, but frequently are the ones used to describe the wisdom and religious revelation coming from sexual "knowing." Walker gives a whole list of such ordinary words from many languages. Some examples are kennen and Konnen in German, ken in Gaelic, gnossco and gnosis in Latin and Greek. Derived from these roots are words such as genital, genetic, genus and engender. Words like cunning, kenning, and ken (knowledge) are all derived from words related to cunt. Kennet, the British Great Goddess's sacred river at Silbury, once was called Cunnit or Cunnt.

To get back to different symbols for the vulva, another name for the double-pointed oval of the "yoni" is the *"vesica piscis,"* the Vessel of the Fish. The ancients connected women and fish symbolically. They felt a woman's sexual secretions smelled like fish.

Joseph Campbell, in *Creative Mythology*, tells us one of the Hindu titles of the Great Goddess was "a virgin named Fishy

Smell, whose real name was Truth." The Chinese Great Mother, Kwan-yin ("Yoni of yonis") often appeared as a fish-goddess. In Greek, the word *delphos* meant both fish and womb. The original Delphic oracle belonged to the pre-Hellenic fish-goddess called Themis. She was often shown as a great fish, whale, or dolphin (dephinos). According to Walker, the ancient Mother, particularly in her love goddess aspect, was associated with fish, seashells, salt, ships and fisherman. In her honor according to Walker, fish were eaten on Friday, her official day, named after Freya, her Scandinavian incarnation. Thus it was, and in some areas still is, believed that fish are an aphrodisiac food.

Imagery which uses a fish as a place of rebirth abounds in ancient art and legends. The legend of Jonah and the whale is only one example. The earliest examples come from the painted caves of 25,000 years ago. From one of these caves, Peche-Merle, I brought home a souvenir showing two horses decorated with dots. In the stomach of one of the horses is the red (color of life) outline of a fish. Later, the *vesica pisces* was also used by the early Christians to draw the symbol in the dirt which identified themselves to each other. Today, the symbol is used to denote membership in the Christian religion.

When the "yoni" passed into Western symbolism it was called a "mandorla" (almond). From the earliest days, almonds, I guess because of their shape, were both a female-genital symbol and a fertility charm. Almonds are referred to both in Exodus 25:33, where there is a description of how to make the menorah, and in Numbers 17:8 where Aaron's flowering staff is described. Modern Jewish Biblical interpretations of these passages refer to the almond tree's pattern of flowering in the spring while its branches are still bare. From this they make the connection to the almond representing fertility and regeneration, which expresses the same ancient idea without the sexual reference. Walker says, in Christian imagery, the mandorla is described as a "gateway"; this also keeps the original meaning without the sexual imagery. Madonnas frequently are shown standing inside a mandorla. A souvenir I brought back from Mexico is a small statue of St. Guadeloupe of Mexico, standing inside of such a shape.

The *vesica piscis* is also the symbol displayed by the figures known as Sheela na Gig, which were found, before they were destroyed, at the entrance of Irish churches built before the 16th century. Today there is still a famous one at the Saints Mary and David Church in Kilpeck near Herford. The Sheela na Gig is an old female figure squatting with her knees apart to display her vulva. Traditionally, as a bride entered the church for her wedding, she rubbed the vulva of the Sheela na Gig for good luck. When I explained this custom to two good Irish Catholic friends, they looked at me in total disbelief and almost in unison said "Not in Ireland, not in the church!" Yet I saw these figures for sale in souvenir shops on the main streets of Dublin. The Sheela na Gig figures closely resemble the yonic statues of Kali, which appear at the doorways of Hindu temples. The cus-

The Sheela na Gig

tom there is for visitors to lick a finger and touch the yoni "for luck." Walker tells us that, from all the touching, some of the older figures have deep holes worn in their yonis.

Another common symbol of the vulva is the cowry shell. According to Joseph Campbell in *Primitive Mythology*, cowries have been found in ancient burial sites all over the world. Some of these graves date as far back as 22,000 years. Scholars believe they were put in graves as a rebirth symbol. Walker tells us they were used throughout the Middle East, Egypt, the South Pacific, and the Mediterranean countries as charms for healing, fertility, rebirth, magical power, or good luck. In the Southwest, I watched Native Americans dancing at a festival wearing strings of cowrie shells. At a stand displaying their wares, these necklaces were among the offered goods. With me was a woman who, until she could see the shape of the opening, had difficulty accepting the idea that at one time the shells were vulva symbols. After she examined the shells herself, the resemblance was so strong she needed no further convincing. Today, Southwest Native Americans say they represent rain. I'm not sure how they get to that symbolism.

Stone Age tombs and barrow-mounds were designed as "wombs" so the dead could be reborn. Their narrow long entrance passages show that Neolithic folk went to considerable trouble to create, in earth and stone, imitations of female anatomy. Newgrange, in the Boyne Valley of Ireland, is the most impressive passage grave I ever climbed through. It is very old, built over 5,000 years ago as part of the religious practices of a pre-Celtic world. To get into it, we first had to work our way through some 37 feet of single file passage; finally we came into a good-sized chamber (about 15 of us were in the party and we could all crowd in). The most fascinating thing, though, about Newgrange is that on the shortest day of the year, the Winter Solstice, the first rays at sunrise enter through a roof box, come down the long passage and strike the very back of the interior chamber. As the sun continues to rise, the whole interior is lit. The Winter Solstice is an important time of the year, as it marks the turning of the year, the end of the old year and the coming of the new. To light the "womb" of a large passage grave is not only a wonderful rebirth and regeneration symbol for the New Year, it also took some pretty fancy engineering and astronomical knowledge to pull off.

To continue the womb imagery, caves and burial chambers were said to be sunk in the "bowels" of the earth—that is, in Mother Earth. In the era of the promiscuous priestesses, the words for cave, temple, and brothel were often interchangeable. Walker says to visit the cave and lie with the "holy harlot" was an act of worship. Later, Christian cathedrals centered on the space called the nave, which originally meant "belly."

In the vegetable world, it seems that all new growth comes out of the dead plants. The ancient religions most likely used this observance to make the connection they developed between life and death. Elinor Gadon, in *The Once and Future Goddess*, says that central to their beliefs was the concept of death and birth as an unbroken continuity of one ever-repeating cycle. As I said earlier, this is very different from our modern idea of birth and death as opposites. When you consider birth and death as parts of a cycle, it becomes clear why many early graves were found covered with a triangular stone or formed in the sign of rebirth, the shape of an egg. Megalithic graves in Western Europe are often in the form of a vagina and uterus.

Tombs have no other purpose than to be sacred resting places for the dead; and these ancient tombs are from the age when death was linked with the idea of rebirth. The word tomb descended from Latin tumulus, which also meant a pregnant belly or a swelling. Eisler tells us that burial mounds, often with a triangular door, provided an imitation of Mother Earth's pregnant belly and "vaginal" passage, through which the dead could be reborn. In many of the early Aegean burials, the tombs were round and the opening into them small. Scholars have wondered why it should be this way. But if the tomb was viewed as a womb for future rebirth, it would make sense to have it round, and if the opening were to represent the vagina, it would be small.

Grottos and caves also were considered the womb of the Earth Mother. Their entrances were the sacred doorways or vaginal openings. This is a natural development when you remember the earth was the body of the Mother Earth. Caves were used as places of initiation and as places to bury the dead. Caves, the womb of the Mother Earth were the first "temples." They were felt to be places of mystical influence and creation. But, unlike the woman's womb, the earth's womb not only brought forth life, but also received back the dead. Many tribal people today, including the Pueblo Indians of the Southwest, believe their first, mythic ancestors emerged from caverns, or mounds in the earth.

According to Dames, certain mythological marriages were also celebrated in caves: for example, the marriage of Jason and Medea, or that of Aeneas and Dido. In the *Aeneid*, Virgil tells us that, at the consummation of the union of Aeneas and Dido, a storm broke out in which the thunder boomed and the lighting flashed, a sign that the God of Heaven was approaching his spouse, the Earth Mother. That's quite a way to celebrate your wedding night! In that world, "sex" very much was what makes the world go round.

Not only were the symbols of sex important in the ancient world, the act of sex was once an important road to mystical or ecstatic states. Eisler tells us, in ancient beliefs, sexual activity provided men with their spiritual nourishment by the act of their "plugging in" to the female power. This not only gave a moment or two of godlike bliss; it also gave the essential contact with the mysterious magic inside a woman's body, which produces new life. Their view was that the sexual act created an altered state of consciousness, which could be a path to spiritual bliss and illumination. Strange as this idea may be to us, it is the basis for the ancient but still existing Indian cult of ecstasy called Tantra. In a display of religious artwork from India, I saw this idea most graphically depicted. The exhibit consisted of male and female deities in an assortment of sexual positions. The idea being represented was that of unity, of wholeness. The group I was with tried hard to be sophisticated and cool with the imagery, but after looking at dozens of the artifacts, we were reduced to the standard modern reaction of giggles and jokes. For us, the thought of such artifacts expressing a religious idea was not only uncomfortable, it was beyond our ability to cope. But as Eisler tells us, in the early days, "sex was integral to the cosmic order." Therefore, the pleasures of sex offered a way of coming closer to the Goddess, not to sin.

We can see, then, as Eisler tells us, that the central themes of both Paleolithic and Neolithic religious are the mysteries of sex, birth, death, and regeneration. These ideas were expressed through sexual images. Although the art historian lecturing on the "Oxbow" painting didn't see it quite that way, it is interesting to note how that form of expression still works.

FOR FURTHER READING

Campbell, Joseph. *Primitive Mythology*. New York: Viking Penguin, 1959. Print.

Eisler, Riane. *Sacred Pleasure*. San Francisco: HarperSanFrancisco, 1995. Print.

Dames, Michael. *The Silbury Treasure: The Great Goddess Rediscovered*. London: Thames and Hudson, 1976. Print.

Eliade, Mircea. *History of Religious Ideas, Vol. I, From the Stone Age to the Eleusinian Mysteries*. Translated: W. Trask. Chicago: Univ. of Chicago Press 1978. Print.

Gimbutas, Marija. *Civilization of the Goddess*. New York: Harper, 1991. Print.

Gadon, Elinor W. *The Once and Future Goddess.* New York: HarperCollins, 1989. Print.

Levy, Gertrude Rachel. *The Gate of Horn.* London: Faber & Faber, 1946. Print.

Moon, Beverly, Ed. *An Encyclopedia of Archetypal Symbolism.* Boston: Shambala, 1991. Print.

Plaut, W. Gunther, Ed. *The Torah, A Modern Commentary.* New York: Union of American Hebrew Congregations, 1981. Print.

Sjoo, Monica, and Mor, Barbara. *The Great Cosmic Mother.* New York: Harper & Row, 1987. Print.

Stone, Merlin. *When God Was a Woman.* New York: Harcourt Brace Jovanovich, 1976. Print.

Walker, Barbara. *The Woman's Dictionary of Symbols & Sacred Objects.* San Francisco: Harper, 1988. Print.

———. *The Woman's Encyclopedia of Myths and Secrets.* San Francisco: HarperSanFrancisco, 1983. Print.

CHAPTER 8

The Story of Oedipus

OLD STORIES FASCINATE ME PRIMARILY BECAUSE, FREquently, there is another story beneath the story being told. Let's look at a well-known oldie. When Robert Graves in his *Greek Myths*, discusses the story of Oedipus, he first tells the traditional tale of Oedipus. Oedipus was the son of King Laius and Queen Iocaste of Thebes. In the story, the Delphic Oracle, the major center for prophecy in ancient Greece, told Laius that any son born of Iocaste would murder him. So, according to the legend, when Oedipus was born Laius either put the baby on a mountaintop or sent him down the river in a chest. But Oedipus didn't die; he was rescued by a shepherd who, according to some of my research, tied his feet together and pierced them with a stake causing his feet to be permanently swollen, which is the meaning of "Oedipus." Also the word "Oedipus" comes from the Greek root meaning knowledge. This is one of those interesting layers that remains a mystery, because no one seems to be able to connect his name into anything that is taking place in the story.

Anyway, the shepherd brought the baby to his master, King Polybus of Corinth, who adopted and raised him. As a young man, Oedipus went to the Delphic Oracle to ask about his future. The Oracle told him he would kill his father and marry

79

his mother. Since Oedipus loved his adoptive parents, he immediately left Corinth. On foot, on the road between Delphi and Daulis, at a triple crossing called the Triple Way, he met King Laius, his biological father.

Triple crossings in Ancient Greece were very significant, since they had a sacred quality to them. When we traveled to Delphi, the tour guide pointed out the very spot where it is believed that this meeting happened. It was really strange to see in front of us the setting of this very ancient story. Anyway, Laius ordered him off the road, which angered Oedipus, and after some words he killed Laius's charioteer. Oedipus then pulled Laius from the chariot and when Laius became entangled in the reins, he was dragged to his death by the horses.

As Graves continues in his story, Laius had been on the way to ask the Oracle how to rid Thebes of the Sphinx, a monster described as having a woman's head, a lion's body, a serpent's tail and eagle's wings. The Goddess Hera had sent the Sphinx to punish Thebes because of an ancient crime. As punishment, the Sphinx asked every traveler to Thebes this riddle: "What has sometimes two feet, sometimes three feet, sometimes four feet and is weakest when it has the most?" Those who couldn't answer the question were throttled and eaten on the spot.

When the Sphinx asked Oedipus the riddle, he easily replied, "Man, because he crawls on all fours as a baby, stands on two feet as an adult and uses a cane in old age." Since this was the correct response that no one else had given, the Sphinx was defeated; she killed herself by throwing herself from the mountain. The grateful Thebans made Oedipus their king, and as was the custom of the time, Oedipus the king, unaware she was his biological mother, married the widow, Queen Iocaste.

A good deal of time passed, but then a plague came to Thebes. When the Delphic Oracle was consulted, the response was "Expel the murderer of Laius." Since Oedipus did not know he was the murderer, he pronounced a curse on Laius's murderer and sentenced him to exile. At this point, the blind seer, Teresias, advised Oedipus that he, Oedipus, was the one who killed Laius, who was his biological father, and married his biological mother. When Iocaste heard this news, she hanged herself for shame and grief. Oedipus blinded himself with a pin taken from Iocaste's garments. Oedipus left the city, eventually dying at Colonus—although Homer has him dying in battle.

You must admit that, in spite of being the name of a Freudian complex and several marvelous plays by Sophocles, Oedipus is a weird story with lots of strange events. What really is going on? To give an explanation, I must digress a bit, step back in time to before 2000 BCE (Before the Common Era) and talk about a world different from ours, with different values and cultures.

In this world of 2000 BCE, and from the very beginning of civilization, women were honored as magical figures who could create, nurture and transform. This was the time when the deity was female and the Goddess reigned. Built into the belief structure of that world were two rituals, which are central and repeat themselves time and time again. They are the ritual sacrifice of the king and the *Hieros Gamos*, the sacred marriage between the queen/priestess and the king/consort. The enactment of these rituals followed the cycles of the season, although, over many thousands of years of observance, there were many variations of timing and practice.

Marija Gimbutas, in *Civilization of the Goddess*, tells us that, in this world where the goddess ruled, the chief personage was the high priestess who, in many cases, was also the queen. There is some belief that the priestess inherited this right by matrilineal descent; that is, she inherited the role from a female of her line, a mother, aunt, whoever. The ruling power was hers; however she did bestow some power to a consort of her choosing. One of the main tasks of the priestess/queen was to enter into the sacred marriage with the consort, who frequently was younger and who was called her son/lover.

On a regular basis, at first annually or semi-annually, the sacrifice of the chosen son/lover who was the king took place. As time went by and the culture changed, the role of the king became more powerful, and the ritual sacrifices of the chosen son/lover/king occurred less frequently. The ritual sacrifices were important to the community because they ensured the fertility of the fields. If the Egyptian story of Osirus and Isis is to be considered the normal sacrifice pattern, the body of the sacrificed king was divided and spread in the fields to ensure fertility. The sacrifice usually took place on the original New Year's Day. In addition to the seasonal sacrifice, ritual sacrifice of the king also took place at signs of his physical weakness or decay. To fulfill his role as a sacred link between the community and the deity, the king had to be perfect physically.

Now, remembering that the above concepts are central to the ancient society, let's return to the story of Oedipus. Graves, in his discussion of the Oedipus story, analyzes a variety of the components of the traditional story.

Graves feels Laius's murder is a straightforward account of a ritual death/sacrifice of the king by his successor. He also feels that, since King Laius was the earthly enactment of the Solar King (the consort of the Lunar Queen), he would be driving the chariot of the Solar King. Tradition stated the successor/slayer must throw him from his chariot and drag him to death by the chariot's horses. The way the story is told, it sounds as if this is what took place outside of Delphi at the junction of the sacred Triple Way. According to Barbara Walker in *The Woman's Encyclopedia of Myths and Secrets*, the Helenes worshiped the goddess Hecate at places where three roads met. Her images guarded three-way crossroads for many centuries; thus she was Hecate Trevia, "Hecate of the Three Ways." Offerings were left at her roadside shrines on nights of the full moon.

To establish his claim to the throne, the new king then must marry the queen, who is also the high priestess. In this tradition, the seat of power is the high priestess. She derives her power from the Great Goddess. According to this explanation, Iocaste is the real power in Thebes. To renew the kingdom and appease the Great Goddess, she regularly offers her son/lover king for sacrifice.

The Sphinx is described as being an animal having a woman's head, lion's body, serpent's tail and eagle's wings. This is a description of the Greek Sphinx, not the more familiar Sphinx of Egypt. Graves feels she is the winged Moon Goddess of Thebes, whose body, according to him, represents the two parts of the Theban year, lion for the waxing part (the winter solstice to the summer solstice), and serpent for the waning part (summer solstice to the winter solstice).

Graves then asks the question, "Was Oedipus a thirteenth century invader of Thebes who suppressed the old Minoan cult of the Goddess and reformed the calendar?" That isn't as wild a leap of fancy as it first appears. Under the old Goddess-worshipping system, even though the new king was a foreigner, the populace considered him to be a son of the old king. It then was correct for him to sacrifice (murder) the old king and marry the Queen. While the Goddess culture has the sacrifice of the king as one of its main rituals, the Indo-European invaders, whose culture didn't sacrifice the king regarded this custom as murder and parricide. This may explain why so many of the old stories involve murdering the father. Graves' timing of the original story as being in the 13th century BCE is based on the great upheavals and movement of that period. While the invasions from the North began many thousands of years earlier, probably around 3500 BCE, it was not until the 13th century BCE that the conquest of the local goddess communities was complete.

Gimbutas discusses the collapse of these Bronze Age goddess culture communities as coinciding with the invasion of the Greek-speaking Indo-Europeans or Aryans. The Indo-Europeans, who worshipped the father gods, came from beyond the Danube and the Black Sea in successive waves. Peter Green, in *Ancient Greece,* says we determine this in a variety of ways, one of the main ones being examination of the words the newcomers borrowed from the local population. Borrowed words include such local nouns as "vine," "olive," "fig," "wheat" and "sea." Such borrowings imply the newcomers came from the inland steppes where such words were not needed. As an indication of the low level of the invaders' civilization, they also borrowed the word for bathtub. Other clues, such as grave remains, myths, and rituals, tell us these tribes not only domesticated the horse, but knew how to ride it. They also developed skills to make a war chariot from a wagon. They were able to keep secret over several centuries their knowledge of making iron tools. They were a warrior society who, according to Joseph Campbell in *Oriental Mythology,* "were polygamous, patriarchal, proud of the genealogies, tent dwellers, filthy and tough." They considered themselves superior, and, eventually totally dominated the old goddess communities. Why they were what they were, why they developed a patriarchal system with male gods, when the rest of the known world was developing along a matrilineal pattern, is just not known. When they came, they took over the old cultures and imposed their own. In most cases they didn't eliminate the Goddess; they reduced Her, diminished Her and made Her values and practices evil.

Graves says in the earliest days, the invasions of the Indo-Europeans, who were the early Greeks, were not terribly destructive to the goddess communities. The invaders were small armed bands of patriarchal herdsman who worshipped the Aryan gods and attached themselves to the pre-Hellenic settlements in Thessaly and Central Greece. The settlements accepted them as children of the local goddess, and used the invaders to provide the goddess with sacred kings.

As time went on, the annual sacrifice of the king became less attractive to the sitting kings. Graves said eventually, the kings were able to stretch the time of their reign from the traditional thirteen-month lunar year to a Great Year of 100 lunations, and then to a nineteen-year period, which is the point where the lunar calendar and the solar calendar merge. However, the sacred king still held his position only by right of marriage. The throne remained the power of the queen/priestess and that power descended matrilineally.

The invasions of 13th BCE seriously weakened the matrilineal tradition. The weakening permitted the king to further extend his reign and move descent from the mothers to the fathers. By the close of the second millennium BCE when the Greek tribes called Dorians arrived, patrilineal succession became the rule.

Now what is the original story of Oedipus? According to Graves, it may once have run something like this:

Oedipus of Corinth conquered Thebes and became king by marrying Iocaste, a priestess of Hera. Afterwards he announced that the kingdom should henceforth be bequeathed from father to son in the male line, which is a Corinthian custom, instead of remaining a gift of Hera the Throttler. (Please note that one of Hera's names is the Throttler and the Sphinx throttled the people of Thebes who couldn't answer the riddle.) Oedipus confessed that he felt himself disgraced at having let chariot horses drag to death Laius, who was accounted his father, and at having married Iocaste, who had enroyalled him by a ceremony of rebirth. But when he tried to change their customs, Iocaste committed suicide in protest, and Thebes was visited by a plague. Upon the advice of an oracle . . . the Thebans banished him. He died in a fruitless attempt to regain his throne by warfare.

You must admit it comes out a different story. It's not as weird a tale as the old one; but to me, it is one that makes a lot more sense. Remember, a lot of the old stories have these layers.

FOR FURTHER READING

Campbell, Joseph. *Oriental Mythology*. New York: Viking Press, 1964. Print.
Gimbutas, Marija. *Civilization of the Goddess*. New York: Harper, 1991. Print.
Graves, Robert. *The Greek Myths*. London: Cassell, 1955. Print.
Green, Peter. *Ancient Greece*. London: Thames and Hudson, 1984. Print.

CHAPTER 9

From the World of Milk and Honey

I FIRST HEARD THE PHRASE "A LAND FLOWING WITH milk and honey" when I was a child. One of my favorite Bible stories was Joshua who, when he returned from scouting the promised land bearing grapes, reported it was a land "flowing with milk and honey" (Numbers 13:7) I always wondered why, if the land was "flowing with milk and honey," they brought back grapes, but who was I to question a Bible story? Imagine my surprise when I learned that the phrase "milk and honey" is scattered about 20 times through the Old Testament. It first shows up in Exodus, where God uses it to describe the land he is promising (Exodus 3:8, 3:17, 33:3, 13:5), and continues being used through Ezekiel 20:15 where Ezekiel is speaking for God. Obviously, it is not a description of a place but a stock phrase used to describe an earthly paradise. Ellen Frankel and Betsy Teutsch, in *The Encyclopedia of Jewish Symbols*, tell us that in the Bible, milk usually symbolizes abundance and fertility. But why is it milk and honey that describe the ultimate Paradise? Monica Sjoo and Barbara Mor, in *The Great Cosmic Mother*, tell us that lands "flowing with milk and honey" were in fact the lands of the Neolithic goddess.

Also in the Bible are blessings made in one of the names of God, Shaddai (Shad is the Hebrew for breast) which invoke

"Blessings of the breast and womb" (Genesis 49:25). Actually, Shaddai is used 48 times in the Old Testament, and when it is used, fruitfulness and fertility are being invoked. Rabbi Arthur Wasko, in the January 15, 2001 edition of *The Jerusalem Report*, tells us that "God is seen as Infinite Mother." For a religion that is as heavily patriarchal as Judaism, this is very strange material. After examining the material, I saw clearly that these feminine Biblical references are from a very ancient time when the deity was female.

The mother's abundant and flowing breast is one of a baby's first experiences. From this is formed one of the basic images in the universe. Even after the destruction of the goddess culture, the power of mother's milk and the breast remained a strong image for humans. According to Erich Neumann in *The Great Mother*, the breast motif involves the symbolism of milk and cow. Barbara Walker, in *The Women's Dictionary of Symbols and Sacred Objects*, says that the goddess as cow is one of the earliest historical motifs of worship, occurring as far back as Mesopotamia and early Egypt.

So, the tradition of milk and honey as sacred foods come from the era of the Goddess communities before the arrival of the patriarchal era. According to Neumann, milk and honey were sacrificed in the oldest times to the earth goddesses. These ancient communities regarded milk and honey, and with them cows and bees, as sacred symbols. Since the last of these communities were destroyed around 1500 BCE (Before the Common Era), we are talking of an earlier time. Because of her milk, the female deity which these communities worshipped became the source of nourishment and abundance. The ancient world considered milk as a miraculous gift from the female.

Walker tells us Greek legend teaches that the Milky Way, the name for our galaxy, was formed when Hera nursed Hercules. He sucked so hard, her milk spurted across the heavens. The word "galaxy" comes from the word *laktos*, which in ancient

Greek meant "mother's milk." Arabians called the Milky Way "Mother of the Sky." The names differ; but all through the ancient world, the Milky Way was regarded as originating from the Goddess's milk. Anne Baring and Jules Cashford, in *The Myth of the Goddess*, say the idea that the moon is made of green cheese goes back to the legend which has the moon being curdled as a ball of cheese from the Milky Way. In the Near East, they thought human bodies were curdled from the Goddess's milk. This idea is found in the story of Job: "Has thou not poured me out as milk, and curdled me like cheese?" (Job 10:10).

The female breast and its milk have always been closely associated with the cow and its milk. As Walker tells us, the cow was one of the earliest and most common images of the Great Goddess. In much of the ancient world, She was symbolized as the white, horned, milk-giving moon-cow. Even today, our language includes phrases such as "Holy Cow" and "Sacred Cow." The very name of the Goddess in different cultures supports the close tie between the Goddess and the cow. Again, as Walker states, in India the Goddess has always been the sacred cow, "Fountain of milk and curds." In Scandinavia, the Cow of Creation was Audumla, whose name means "Creator of the Earth." The name of the biblical matriarch Leah means "Wild Cow," which is a title of the Mesopotamian Goddess. In Greece, the Goddesses Hera and Io each took the form of a cow. Hera was once the mother of the pastures, and cows regularly were sacrificed to her. The goddess Io was the white cow-goddess, the Moon. In Egypt, Isis-Hathor was the divine kau (cow) from whose udder came the Milky Way and all the stars. Hathor, who was the Great Mother of Egypt, was portrayed either as a cow or with the head and horns of a cow. One of Hathor's Greek names was Europa, mother of the continent of Europe. Europa's name means "Full Moon," and she was wedded to the father of gods in the form of a white bull. J. C. Cooper, in *Sym-*

bolic and Mythological Animals, tells us the cow appears frequently in Celtic mythology as a provider of nourishment for entire communities, like the magic cows of Manannan, one speckled, one dun with twisted horns who were always in milk. Cows are frequent in otherworld imagery, with magic and supernatural powers.

What's more, the name Italy means "calf-land." Some years ago on a flight to Italy I picked up a packet of milk. Written on it was the word "latte," milk in Italian. This was well before you could pick up a "latte" at any corner coffee shop. Knowing this, I was not surprised when Walker said that the Etruscans, who were the ancient Italians, felt their country was the gift of the Milk-giver, whom they called Lat, whom the Arabs call Al-Lat, while the Greeks called her Latona, Lada, Leta, or Leda. This goddess ruled Laatium, and gave her milk (latte) to the world. A favorite Roman emblem of the Goddess was the Cornucopia, the Horn of Plenty, which is a cow's horn pouring forth all the fruits of the earth.

An ancient community that gives a clear picture of the sacredness of milk and mother's breast is Minoan Crete. Crete, until its destruction and conquest around 1500 BCE, was the last of the Great Goddess communities. As far as we know, it was also one of the most developed and important communities. The Great Goddess of Minoan Crete is familiar to anyone who has leafed through books of ancient art. Statues and paintings show her standing in a flounced skirt with bare breasts, holding coiling snakes in both hands. Much of the commentary in these books refers to the elegant style of the dress. Yet in Crete, the uncovering of the breast was not a fashion statement but a sacred gesture of the cult. The Goddess, and the priestesses identified with Her, show their full breasts as symbols of the nourishing life stream of the Mother. Walker tells us that in all the Goddess communities, touching and pressing the breasts was an important statement of belief.

The Snake-Goddess of Minoan Crete

The power of this image continued even after the communities were destroyed. Some examples are found in artwork as late as the Middle Ages. In Medieval paintings, according to James Hall in *Dictionary of Subjects and Symbols in Art*, St. Bernard in several paintings is shown kneeling before the Virgin. She is pressing her breast from which milk spurts, symbolically wetting the saint's lips. I once I saw a painting like this. It was some years ago, while I was wandering through the Gothic paintings at the Uffizi in Florence, Italy. In the painting, I saw the young woman who was pressing her breast was on the right, her milk streamed out in an arc to the mouth of the kneeling bearded man on the left side of the painting. To my 20th century eyes, this is a very strange painting. Yet it clearly demonstrates the power of the imagery of both milk and breast. While I have searched through the literature looking for the painter or the name of the painting, I come up blank, Yet when

St. Bernard receiving a spray of milk from the Virgin's breast

I describe the scene most people who have been there say, "Oh yes, I remember that painting." It's an image that stays with us a long time.

All of these paintings represent woman as nurturer, as a giver of riches. Societies whose main image is one that reaches out to nurture, to care for, should be societies that value caring and nurturing. From what we have learned about Minoan Crete, it appears this was so. Riane Eisler, in *The Chalice and the Blade*, tells us theirs was a world of abundance, joy, peace, pleasure, and wealth. It was a world in which the symbols of milk and honey abounded. According to Baring and Cashford, the Great Goddess of Crete was closely connected to the bee as well as the breast. From Crete, not only are there artifacts of the Goddess offering her breasts, but also ones of her as a bee.

Okay, I understand milk being of Paradise, but what is the role of honey? Honey was the only sweetener of the ancient world. Neumann tells us that, in ancient days, honey was sacrificed to the earth goddesses. The bee was rightly looked up to as a symbol of the feminine power of nature. It was associated above all with the Goddesses, Demeter, Artemis and Persephone. Bees appear in the spring, at the rebirth of grasses and flowers. All of this helps explain how the bee came to be the symbol of the female deity and, as such, an expression of rebirth. Honey features in rites of regeneration. It was used in Mesopotamian cults at the dedication of new images and in the New Year (Akitu) ritual, and is still eaten by Jews at the New Year.

From earliest times, honeyed milk was associated with birth and initiation rituals. It was the food of babies, initiates, kings and priests. Theodore Gaster, in *Myth, Legend, and Custom*, tells us that, in the Old Testament, honey and milk curd was the characteristic food of newborn babes. He then lists Zeus and Dionysus as examples of this first nurturing. Both Arabs and Jews, immediately after birth, smeared date juice or honey on a baby's gums. The Greeks said that when the God Dionysus was born, honey was smeared on his lips. The Hindus do the same thing as soon as they cut the umbilical cord. The head chief of the Masai tribes of Africa could eat nothing but milk, honey, and the roasted livers of goats. They believed if he ate any other food he would lose his magical powers. This idea even made its way into the Bible. In Isaiah 7:14–15, we are told that a young woman shall bear a son named Immanuel who will eat curd and honey so that he may refuse evil and choose the good.

My investigation deepened when I learned bees, and therefore honey, were scarce in ancient Israel. Frankel and Teutsch tell us that in the Bible, honey usually refers to a thick syrup made from dates, figs or grapes, but not to bee's honey, which is much more rare in that region. Another explanation might be that since bees are not "kosher," the Israelites at that time could not eat either the bee or its product, honey. This might explain why they used a thick syrup made of chopped dates or figs instead of honey. Why would honey be so important that, if you didn't have it, you had to create something you could call honey? A nursing mother editing my research maintained that the answer is basic. According to her, mother's milk is sweeter than other animal milks. Therefore, using cow's or goat's milk as a ritual substitute for mother's milk required the animal milk to be sweetened. Since honey was the only sweetener of the time, honey would be used. In this way, the animal milk with honey became the sacred substitute for mother's milk, the first food for human babies. This sounds reasonable to me, but nothing in the literature suggests such a relationship. Of course, the literature is not written by nursing mothers, so maybe this point got lost.

Honey also played a central part in the New Year rituals at Crete. According to Baring and Cashford, the Cretan New Year culminated on July 20, when the great star Sirius rose with the sun. In these countries, Sirius was the star of the Goddess. The rising of Sirius ended a forty-day ritual. During this time, honey was gathered from the hives of the bees in the caves and the woods. The honey was then fermented into the alcoholic beverage called mead, which was drunk as part of the New Year rites. Jane Harrison, in *Prolegomena to the Study of Greek Religion*, tells us that mead, which was naturally fermented honey, was one of the first alcoholic beverages. It was developed before wine was. Nectar, the ancient drink of the gods, is also mead made of honey. Plutarch says mead was used as a libation before the appearance of the vine, and "even now those of the barbarians who do not drink wine drink honey-drink."

Sjoo and Mor say that the Goddess communities saw the structure of the bee world, with its order and industry, to be the model pattern for the structure of their own world. As Baring and Cashford describe it, bee-keeping was a metaphor for settled agriculture and for the peaceful abundance of the earth. They gave their priestesses, diviners and prophetesses names which mean "bee." For example the priestesses of the Great Goddess, Demeter, were called Melissae, "bees." The chief oracular priestess at Delphi was the Pythia who was called the Delphic Bee. Her emblem as a bee appears on Delphic coins. In ancient Israel, there was Deborah, whose name means Queen Bee and who some suggest was a former matriarchal ruler. At Ephesus, where the many-breasted Artemis-Diana was worshipped, the bee was her cult animal. Her temple at Ephesus was a symbolic beehive (built by priestesses and known as one of the wonders of the ancient world). Her priestesses were called Melissa (bees), and the eunuch priests were Essenes (drones). The officials at the Greek Eleusis Mystery were called Bees. The bee was a sign of the Great Goddess. As the Great Goddess, the bee was a symbol of birth, death and resurrection. The humming of the bee was called the "voice of the goddess," the sound of creation.

Baring and Cashford write that the Greek Pythagoreans felt mathematics was the voice of the order of the universe, and therefore sacred. They worshipped bees as sacred creatures because of the perfect hexagons the bees made in their honeycombs. In the hexagonal shape of honeycombs, the Pythagoreans saw the spirit of Aphrodite, whose sacred number was six (the dual Triple Goddess).

In many cultures, honey, the mysterious and natural product of bees, is a symbol of rebirth or personal growth. According to Frankel and Teutsch, for centuries, Jews have used honey to mark two important occasions of change and personal development: Rosh Hashanah, the New Year, and the beginning of a child's education. European Jews (Ashkenazi) always have apples dipped in honey on the Rosh Hashanah table, as well as honey cake, to symbolize hope for a sweet New Year. Beginning in the Middle Ages until our own day, it has been a custom to write the Hebrew alphabet in honey on a slate when a child begins to study the Torah. This symbolizes the parents' hope that the child will find the words of the Torah as sweet as honey and that in turn, the child will make its teachings fruitful.

As I was researching this material back in 1994, I learned of the controversial gathering of some 2,000 churchwomen from some of the major Protestant denominations. They had come together spiritually to approach God in a way meaningful for women. Six months later, the involved denominations were still coping with negative repercussions from the gathering. Among the things the women did which upset church officials, was sharing milk and honey as part of a prayer extolling female sexuality. Without dealing with the sexuality aspect, the custom of ritually sharing milk and honey was part of the ancient Christian church. In the early days of the church, the ritual order had Baptism immediately following Communion; and those who had just been baptized drank, not only wine, but also a cup of mixed milk and honey. This goes back to the idea of milk and honey being associated with birth and initiation rituals. So while the tradition of drinking milk and honey did exist in the early church, its ritual use is from a time much earlier than Christianity. It's easy to see why the officials were disconcerted.

It seems to me to be very clear that milk and honey had the same sacred function in the days of the Goddess as bread and wine hold in our current world. There is something very comforting and reassuring about unlimited amounts of milk being shared that bread and wine misses. Of course, I also like the idea that it is feminine.

FOR FURTHER READING

Baring, Anne, and Cashford, Jules. *The Myth of the Goddess*. New York: Penguin, 1991. Print.

Cooper, J. C. *Symbolic and Mythological Animals*. Wellingborough, Northamptonshire, England: Aquarian Press, 1992. Print.
Eisler, Riane. *The Chalice and the Blade*. New York: Harper & Row, 1988. Print.
Frankel, Ellen, and Teutsch, Betsy Platkin. *The Encyclopedia of Jewish Symbols*. Northvale, NJ: Jason Aronson Inc., 1992. Print.
Gaster, Theodore. *Myth, Legend, and Custom in the Old Testament*. New York: Harper & Row, 1969. Print.
———. *Thespis*. New York: Gordian Press, 1975. Print.
Hall, James. *Dictionary of Subjects and Symbols in Art*. New York: Harper & Row, 1974. Print.
Harrison, Jane. *Prolegomena to the Study of Greek Religion*. Princeton, NJ: Princeton University Press, 1991. Print.
Levy, Gertrude Rachel. *The Gate of Horn*. London: Faber & Faber, 1948. Print.
Neumann, Erich. *The Great Mother*. Princeton, NJ: Princeton University Press, 1963. Print.
Sjoo, Monica, and Mor, Barbara. *The Great Cosmic Mother*. New York: Harper & Row, 1987. Print.
Walker, Barbara. *The Woman's Dictionary of Symbols & Sacred Objects*. San Francisco: HarperSanFrancisco, 1988. Print.
———. *The Woman's Encyclopedia of Myths and Secrets*. New York: HarperCollins, 1983. Print.

CHAPTER 10

Pots and Cauldrons

About 15 years ago, I heard an archeologist from Jordan speak about his excavation site, Zeiraqoun, a 5,000-year-old city in Northern Jordan. His lecture was fascinating, complete with wonderful slides of artifacts he found at the site. One slide was particularly interesting. It showed a clay figurine of a woman, but where the head should have been, there was a pot. The lecturer kept mentioning that, even today, this was a very typical sight in that part of the world, that is, a woman carrying a pot on her head. When I mentioned the figure had no head but only a pot, he really was surprised. Obviously he never looked closely at his slide. But the big question to me was, what does it mean when an ancient feminine figurine has a pot for a head? For all my searching, I never found the exact answer to that question. But I did learn a lot about pots.

The first thing I learned about pots came from Erich Neumann who, in *The Great Mother*, tells us that "The experience of the body as a vessel is universally human" and from the earliest days of human life, pots have always represented the female. It is the round shape of the pots, which looks like a belly or maybe a breast, that made them come to represent the female. In addition, Neumann tells us that a pregnant woman's belly is a container for change, in the same way pots used for cooking are containers for change.

Neumann then connects women to the earth, because earth, also, is a place of change. The way we think of earth as "Mother Earth" certainly is an example of this. It is from these ideas Neumann establishes the view that the pot is a symbol of the female deity. So while a pot is a basic household implement used for all kinds of domestic chores, according to Neumann, that seems to be only part of the story.

Barbara Walker, in her *Women's Dictionary of Symbols and Sacred Objects*, tells us that clay was the basic pot-making material of the ancients. Since clay comes from the earth, which was considered feminine, its use increased the pot/woman symbolism. Also she tells us that, in the mythology of the ancient world, clay pots occurred everywhere as symbolizing human beings, souls, or divine persons. Examples are in Cyprus, where pots called *kernophorai* were worshipped as goddesses, or with ancient Celtic clay pots, crudely marked with human faces which represented either the souls of the dead or the deities of wherever the dead went. In India, a black pot was the symbol of the Goddess Kali. Farmers hung such pots in their fields to avert the evil eye from their crops. Also in India, there was a creating-and-destroying goddess called Kali Ma, with a special incarnation as Kel Mari, the Pot Goddess. Since she made the first man out of clay, her people were Aryans, from arya "man of clay." Kali's other name, Maya, was the same name as the Central American civilization whose women produced remarkable pottery. Neither I, nor anybody else as far as I can find, has any explanation as to how the name for the pot goddess of India got to South America. The oldest form of Mayan pottery was known as Mamom, "the Grandmother." Early Greek and early Egyptian pottery, until the introduction of the potter's wheel, was also woman-made. The biblical God's creation of Adam out of clay was taken from ancient scriptures of the Potter-Goddess, whose creative substance was *adamah* ("bloody-clay").

The next thing I learned about pots was that they were seen as magical. Neumann tells us that the ancients considered all of the everyday things we do which involve changing something from one thing to another—like cooking, sewing, potmaking or building houses—as mysteries of great power. Included in the mysteries as well were all of Nature's natural changes, such as the seasons changing. These mysteries all belonged to the "secret province of the Feminine." As a result, these changes contained a spiritual character, which was more than the mere "technical" process. The vessels and pots used in the magical process of changing things, whether by cooking and fermenting, or making medicine, poison, or intoxicants, became part of the magic. Jars, kettles, and ovens are examples of vessels with a belly character, which made them magical. Women, but only women, were part of the magic, because only women, through their ability to create babies, were also magical vessels. It is in this way the ancients made a connection between mortal women and the Great Goddess. This is why it is the female, whether it is the priestess, or later the witch, who are always holding the magical cauldron or pot. If you question this connection of pots to the female belly, a quick trip through any museum displaying ancient pots with their decorations of breasts and belly makes the idea clear.

I have looked at the ancient pots in museums all over the world, including one in China, and I am struck by how much alike they are. They not only have very much the same shapes, which I suppose could be expected, but they all seem to display very much the same decorative markings. Marija Gimbutas, in *The Language of the Goddess*, sees these patterns of parallel, serpentine or wavy lines and zigzags, spiral and M signs as symbols of the goddess's rain, milk or water. Chevrons, according to Gimbutas, symbolize the wings or beak of a bird, birds in flight or the rippling wake made by a bird moving through water. She adds that the V of the chevron is also a hieroglyph for the genital triangle, and for the life that emerged from the goddess's womb. It is as if, when they made their pots, each community all over the world expressed the same ideas. I find this amazing. The large number and variety of ancient pots made to look like the female body clearly demonstrate this idea. Now, when I see in a museum display a carefully-crafted and elaborately-decorated pot with a sign that says "pot with decorative markings," I get somewhat upset with how they are missing the point.

Sometimes, in order to emphasize the vessel character of the feminine, Walker tells us the ancients used a pot to represent woman. Thus the pot with some type of ornament on the goddess or priestess's head probably came from an actual jar that the goddess or priestess carried on her head during a ritual. In other words, in ancient artifacts, when you see a pot held on the head, or in front of the body, or sometimes beside it, you usually can interpret it as a sacral vessel, used in a religious ritual. Maybe this is the explanation of the Jordanian figurine of a lady with the pot where her head should be. I never found one that was better.

Another thing I learned from Walker is that women were the original potters. Among all primitive peoples, it is the women who make the pots. Only later does pottery-making become a man's occupation. Neumann tells us that, throughout North America, Central and South America, and in those parts of the Malay Archipelago and Peninsula, Melanesia, and New Guinea where pottery making is still practiced as a native industry, it is done exclusively by women.

In ancient times, the really large pots called cauldrons were normally were used daily for heating, boiling or cooking. Their main use was to cook food. However, they can also produce the diabolical or magic potions of the Devil's or witches' cauldrons of legend. Barbara Walker, in *The Crone*, describes the cauldron as the source of life, wisdom, inspiration, understanding and magic. It was an important and central symbol in pagan religion.

I also learned from Walker that cauldrons were the prime female symbol of the pre-Christian world, which is why Christians universally associated them with witchcraft. According to Walker, there can be no doubt that the cauldron represented the womb of the Great Goddess. Like any symbol of vast antiquity, it has acquired complex and far-reaching interpretations through the millennia. Always, the cauldron was understood to signify the cosmic womb, source of regeneration and rebirth.

Male writers often tried to disguise the earlier meanings of the cauldron and/or its contents, because these meanings would not serve the interests of the patriarchies and emerging male-dominant religions. The cauldron concept of eternally recycling life was inevitably opposed to the patriarchal linear concept. Christian tradition has very carefully concealed the theological meaning of the cauldron in the old religions.

The cauldron is a universal symbol, which turns up in Celtic, Egyptian and Chinese myths to name but a few. According to Walker, it symbolized creation, which occurred not just once, as in the Bible story, but constantly. It always stood for the source of regeneration and rebirth, the cosmic womb. The cauldron represented the power of the Goddess, which was part of each act of creation. Everything was created by and in the Goddess and then at death returned to Her. In Her ever-boiling cauldron of regeneration, all the various forms of matter and energy dissolved and mingled in the boiling, so the elements that made all things were separated and then recombined. In a somewhat different wording, this is the concept of matter and energy most modern scientists propose.

There were large cauldrons standing in the ancient Egyptian temples called *shi*. Babylonian temples had the same type of vessel, called an *apsu* or "abyss" which was used for baptism, ceremonial washing, and rebirth rituals. Such a "sea" was also called "the Deep," *tehom* in Hebrew. Solomon's temple contained such a huge tank (Kings 7:23). A footnote in my Jewish Publication Society Bible says the literal translation for tank was "belly" which certainly sounds to me as if Solomon's tank connected to the ancient ideas of a Cauldron of Regeneration. Like the Christian baptismal font, which is descended from these forerunners, the cauldron or "sea" was a womb symbol.

In the Middle Ages, with the dominance of Christianity, paganism went underground and took the cauldron with it. A cauldron represented the medieval housewife as certainly as an ax represented the woodsman and a bow the hunter. The cauldron was one of the most useful articles in the kitchen. Nothing could have been more appropriate as an emblem of the woman of the house. It was essential for cooking, brewing, processing all kinds of food and medicines, treating hides, washing, dyeing, making household items like soap and candles and carrying fire or water. Its use, then, could not be forbidden or banned and removed, like the altars and other images of the pagan temple. Cauldrons were always there. Secret ceremonies involving the cauldron could then take place in spite of church or political restrictions, which according to Walker is why the cauldron figured in popular ideas about witches. Salic Law, the law of the Franks in the sixth century, specifically condemned people who "carried the cauldron" to such meetings.

Celtic folklore is full of tales about a miraculous cauldron. One aspect common to all Celtic cauldrons is that they always were involved with women, the three Muses or the Ninefold Muse—the Goddess in one of her three forms, maiden, mother or crone. Always, it is a cauldron of inspiration and plenty, a source of nourishment and renewal of life. It is a female symbol whether it is the womb, which nourishes and brings forth new life, or the breast, which feeds and nurtures. The name Cerridwen, from Welsh legend, has been translated both as cauldron of wisdom and fortress of wisdom, *caer* meaning fortress, *cerru* meaning cauldron. As Walker tells us, nearly every European country inherited hidden legends of a lost miraculous vessel, the source of life or of enlightenment.

Remember the opening scene of Shakespeare's play *Macbeth*? The play opens with three witches stirring a cauldron and predicting trouble in the future. This scene sets the stage for the action that follows, which is a classic example of how the magic pots or cauldrons worked. Shakespeare, by using this opening, followed the old tradition of using the cauldron and witches to tell the future. As Walker tells us, he also followed tradition by using three witches, who were part of the tradition of the cauldron. From the earliest days in the Bronze Age and Iron Age cultures, the cauldron stood for the Triple Goddess of fate, or *wyrd* in Old English. The Egyptian hieroglyph of the great female Deep (womb), which gave birth to the universe and the gods, was a design of three cauldrons. A worldwide look at myths reveals that the cauldron symbolized the cosmic mother-body, variously located in heaven, in the earth, in the sea, or at times on the moon.

This symbolism carries over to include all kinds of vessels such as cups, dishes and chalices. I was surprised to learn that scholars today believe the traditions of the lost Last Supper chalice, which Christians called the Holy Grail, are not real. According to Walker, the vessel was entirely pagan and feminine, another transformation of the Celtic Cauldron of Regeneration. Although the paganism of the legends was concealed under a thin coating of Christian reinterpretation, they show their paganism and feminine orientation at every turn in the romances. For example, in the Grail stories, the sacred procession appeared in a fairy queen's castle, not in a church, and the holy vessel was always carried by a maiden, not a priest. Behind its almost exaggeratedly Christian exterior, Jean Markale, author of *The Women of the Celts*, tells us, the search for the Grail is really just a vast pagan epic.

As Malcolm Godwin describes it in *The Holy Grail*, at the turn of the tenth century, a strange wave of hysteria swept the Christian world. According to the beliefs of the Christian community, the world should have ended by the year 1000, bringing the long-awaited New Kingdom of Heaven. But instead of the promised paradise on earth, the people found themselves in a bleak and hopeless world. Although the Crusaders took Jerusalem, they promptly lost it. Christian armies were proving no match for the "Infidels," who appeared to have a far more civilized and wondrous culture than their own. It was an age of turmoil, full of experiment and oppression, faith and heresy. This was the era that produced the Grail stories.

According to Godwin, it was not surprising the Grail stories developed during this time. The first groups of Crusaders to the Holy Land were returning, not only with the Infidel's ways, but also with new and revolutionary ideas. This was a time when political power in Europe was fragmented; armed bands roamed the countryside, turning farms into wasteland. In the last decade of the eleventh century, even the weather turned against the poor, with ruined crops, a crippling famine and terrible diseases. The price of land dropped disastrously which made going on a Crusade to rich and booty-laden paradises quite attractive, a pursuit that was encouraged by the priests in Rome who saw advantage in a truly spiritual quest. It was in this highly charged religious atmosphere that the legend of the Grail was born.

The Legend of the Grail first appeared at the end of the twelfth century. It sprang from the head of a gifted poet called Chretien de Troyes. With these stories, we enter the sphere of the marvelous. Godwin tells us the mystery of the Holy Grail gave the Middle Ages the symbol of the journey, which is inward. In these stories, each must find his own way; there is no right way or wrong way to do the journey; each must find his own path. The chalice, vessel, cup, dish and stone that are the primary images of the Grail stories bring forth the concept of the Feminine, which becomes the inspiration, guide and goal of the knights' inner quest. Walker tells us that, even when the Cauldron of Regeneration entered Christian tradition as the Holy Grail, the chalice used at Christ's last supper, it was referred to as an *escuele* or "cauldron."

After several centuries of fervent interest in the stories of the Grail cycle, the feminine connotations of the holy vessel began to show through in various ways. Almost overnight, the stories stopped coming. In fifteenth-century Brunswick, there was an important popular festival called the Grail, held every seven years. It was outlawed in 1481. The fact that the stories were suppressed is not surprising, as they are quite incompatible with Christian theology and its system of postmortem reward and punishment. The myths prophesied that, without the beneficent influence of the Grail (or Cauldron), Europeans would become alienated from the principle of fertility, and bring on the terrible condition known as "the Waste Land." According to Walker, the Cauldron/Grail represented cycles and recurrences, not linear heaven-or-hell choices made once for all time.

From earliest days all over the world—and for that matter still—pots, cauldrons and cups are major symbols expressing the idea of the mystery and psychic unknown. Even today, we speak of "inwardness" and of "inner" values to mean psychic or spiritual contents, as if we hold these values inside our body-vessel. Whatever symbol seems correct to you, keep in mind that the symbol of the sacred vessel as an object of power and as a cause of miraculous events is as old as the existence of the humble pot. I guess that is why having a pot instead of a head on the lady made a good statement of belief. That belief comes from deep inside our human psyches and has been around since the earliest humans.

FOR FURTHER READING

Baring, Anne, and Cashford, Jules. *The Myth of the Goddess*. New York: Penguin, 1991. Print.
Cirlot, J. E. *A Dictionary of Symbols*. New York: Philosophical Library, Inc., 1962. Print.
Ferguson, Diana. *The Magickal Year: A Pagan Perspective on the Natural World*. London: B.T. Batsford Ltd., 1996. Print.
Gimbutas, Marija. *The Language of the Goddess*. New York: Harper & Row, 1989. Print.
Goodrich, Norma Lorre. *Priestesses*. New York: HarperPerennial, 1989. Print.
Godwin, Malcolm. *The Holy Grail: Its Origins, Secrets and Meaning Revealed*. New York: Barnes & Noble Books, 1998. Print.
Harding, M. Esther. *Woman's Mysteries, Ancient & Modern*. Boston: Shambala, 1990. Print.
Howard-Gordon, Frances. *Glastonbury, Maker of Myths*. Glastonbury, Somerset, England: Gothic Image Publication, 1997. Print.
Markale, Jean. *Women of the Celts*. Rochester, Vermont: Inner Tradition Int. Ltd., 1986. Print.
Matthews, John. *The Grail: Quest for the Eternal*. London: Thames and Hudson Ltd., 1981. Print.
Neumann, Erich. *The Great Mother*. Princeton, NJ: Princeton University Press, 1974. Print.
Walker, Barbara. *The Crone*. San Francisco: HarperSanFrancisco, 1985. Print.
———. *The Woman's Dictionary of Symbols & Sacred Objects*. San Francisco: HarperSanFrancisco, 1988. Print.
———. *The Woman's Encyclopedia of Myths and Secrets*. San Francisco: HarperSanFrancisco, 1983. Print.

CHAPTER 11

Way of the Way

DURING EASTER WEEK EACH YEAR, THERE ARE ALWAYS stories in the papers telling of various religious processions following the "Way of the Cross" or "Stations of the Cross." These processions symbolically mark the places where the events that led to Jesus' crucifixion happened. In Jerusalem, the procession stops at what is believed are the actual places of these events. In other places, groups create their own "Way," sometimes outside the church, but sometimes the sacred path celebrated by the priest and congregation is made by taking a circuit of the church and ending inside the church, at the altar.

The idea of the "Way" developed from the belief of the ancients that everything on earth, including the earth itself, was alive and pulsating with energy. They saw the Earth as the body of the Goddess. As a result, following a "Way" in one of its many forms is one of the oldest acts of human worship. Mariea-Gabriele Wosein, in her book *Sacred Dance, Encounter with the Gods*, says that circumambulation of sacred mountains, trees, temples and shrines is one of the oldest of religious activities. It seems these processions began back in the Stone Age when the deity worshipped was the Great Mother. Since early people saw the earth itself as divine, traveling the earth in a procession was an act of worship. As G. Rachel Levy, in the *The Gate of Horn*, observed, early people thought of the divine body as "the road traveled by itself and its seeker."

J. E. Cirlot tells us, in *A Dictionary of Symbols*, every procession is a rite which illustrates the idea of the cycle and of time passing, as is proved by the procession's return to the point of departure. Beverly Moon, in *An Encyclopedia of Archetypal Symbolism*, says one of the most common forms of processions in a "Way" is circumambulation, or walking around something to demonstrate its sacredness. By walking around what is set apart—mountains, trees, temples and shrines—the holy (inside) is separated from the profane (outside). Inside, the holy part is safe, outside is chaos. Yet, by being on the boundary of the two worlds, a person can be in touch with both worlds. Even the paths to the sacred areas are sacred; pilgrimages were and still are made to renew contact with both the holiness of the path, and the sacred power of the site.

According to John Lundquist in his book *The Temple*, the ritual of the procession is the main means of making communication possible between humans and the powers beyond immediate human life. It is the process through which we make contact with these powers. According to Lundquist, we really don't know how ritual is developed or where it comes from. But one of the most basic ritual movements is circumambulation because it represents totality, perfection and taking (inner, spiritual) possession.

Another common type of ritual movement is to walk upward, which can be related to the journey up the sacred mountain or to descend, which is related to the experience of the cave. A third type is walking inward, to the interior of a sanctuary, where the most holy place is to be found. Other forms of ritual movement may include dance, speech and vigorous body movement.

Erich Neumann, in *The Great Mother*, called ritual "the archetype of the way." The kind of ritual he was talking about is not the dry and meaningless one we frequently experience in the Western World. It was a very serious experience, which people felt gave access to spiritual power. To the ancients it was not possible to be casual when enacting a ritual addressed to divine powers. For guidance on how to proceed, one had to look to the past, to the written tradition, and to the authorized masters who, in the past, have received such knowledge. All of the details of the ritual, the method of approach, the way in which the process is done, are important and must be done in the traditional manner. While in the great religious traditions change does take place, for the most part it is viewed with suspicion, especially if it is imposed from outside the traditional structures of authority.

Following a way is supposed to be difficult. According to Neumann, the difficulty was part of the journey. He referred to the "hard and dangerous way" as an archetype. He tells us that as far as we know, this archetype first appeared among the prehistoric men of the Ice Age. In that era, in the area of the world where France and Spain meet, are found the most extraordinary caves in the world. These are the painted caves, which were created by humans just like you and me some 20,000 to 30,000 or more years ago. Deep inside, the walls of these dark mysterious caves are covered with wondrous paintings of animals and symbols. To me though, the most puzzling question was why they are so far inside and why it is so difficult to get to the paintings. Getting to them requires much climbing through difficult terrain, much walking and coping, difficult today even with electric lights and marked paths. Thirty thousand years ago, to get to the paintings had to be a major hazard. According to Neumann, this was the first "way" and this is what a way was supposed to be.

Theodore Gaster, in *Myth, Legend and Custom in the Old Testament*, tells us that in Semitic antiquity, the Akkadian word used was *saharu* which means "to resort to a shrine, perform cultic practices, worship" but which literally means "to circuit" and probably referred in the first place to ritual circumambulation. Similarly, in ancient south Arabian inscriptions, a not-uncommon term for "altar" or "cultic standing stone" is q-y-f or m-q-f, the literal meaning of which is "object of circuit," while a prominent feature of pre-Islamic worship was the rite known as *tawwaf*, in which the altar was solemnly circuited. As with so much of primitive usage, the idiom may be rude and antiquated, but the content is profound and meaningful. As Gaster says "the holy must be protected by a spiritual cordon *sanitaire*, and that cordon must be provided by human beings who are on their feet and moving."

Avebury in England is one of the most baffling "Ways" I have ever seen. I've been there twice, found it fascinating, but missed the point both times. The problem with figuring out Avebury is its size. It's huge; so unless you know what you are looking at (and I didn't), all you see is a collection of enormous stones placed around an area. The area is so large that inside the Avebury circle is a small village with a pub where we ate lunch.

It's located a pleasant drive from London in Wiltshire, about 17 miles from another of England's famous ancient sites, Stonehenge. But while Stonehenge was built a few hundred years after Avebury, Avebury's stone circle dwarfs Stonehenge, as it is the largest stone circle found in England. The whole area is the sacred center of megalithic (great stone) culture in Britain. Scholars date Avebury in the New Stone Age period, about 2600 BCE (Before the Common Era) which makes it 4,600 years old. In England, this was the era of Great Goddess worship.

What the stones at Avebury mark is a processional avenue or "Way." What is difficult to figure out is what it meant. None of the explanations or guidebooks about Avebury or the nearby sites felt right, until I found the work of British archeologist Michael Dames, *The Avebury Cycle*. His explanation was so different from everyone else's that my first reaction was total disbelief. Yet I soon realized his was the only explanation that fit the concept of the earth being the body of the Goddess. He feels the monuments of Avebury are part of the most important Stone Age group in Britain. He maintains that there is general agreement among archeologists that the avenue was intended as a processional way between two monuments whose functions cannot be explained—a wavy line joining two mysteries.

He describes a 37-mile landscape shaped to create an outline of the body of the Great Goddess. To follow this outline is to travel over the entire outline of the body of the Goddess. Every hill, mound, stone, and long barrow was believed to form part of Her maternal body. The ancients connected each season to a body part. Eventually, monuments were erected at significant parts. At each of these monuments, which the ancients regarded as living characters, the ancients celebrated some part of the annual life cycle of the Great Mother. The entire group of monuments was created to celebrate the annual life cycle of the Great Goddess. Each of the monuments not only marks a part of Her body, but each also stands by itself as a separate sacred site with its own special meaning, siting, or folk tales. According to Dames, the outline was formed thousands of years ago, before the monument of Avebury itself was built. The next time I go to England, I can see I'm in for a long hike.

The little piece of the outline of the Goddess's body I saw was the collection of stones at the village of Avebury. Dames described this area as a great avenue located at the Goddess's genitals. Scattered over the landscape near Avebury were other monuments used at different seasons of the year. As the year progressed, the Goddess was born, grew into maiden and lover, became a mother, and turned into the old hag of death. During the course of the year, the monuments took turns to mark the proper season, as well as the proper point in the Goddess's life. The avenue at Avebury, according to Dames, was the site of an annual major May Day procession to urge the Goddess to be fruitful so life could continue on earth. Dames reminds us that, before the invention of writing, people used objects, including buildings, to focus their most important thoughts and beliefs. That might explain the tremendous amount of energy and time which the ancients spent creating this gigantic religious site.

It's really rather remarkable to think that 4,600 years ago, humans not only had thought this concept through, but also had developed the necessary engineering skills to manage the hundreds of enormous stones needed to construct this sacred site. At Avebury, the two great avenues, with 100 pairs of standing stones, are more than a mile and a half long. The sheer size and width of the processional avenues suggest that, whatever ceremonies and rites were conducted at Avebury, a great many people were involved. Something very important was taking place there.

Another exciting ancient "Way," actually the first one I ever saw, which was as the kids would say "awesome," are the avenues of undressed (left in their natural state) granite stones that stretch across the plains around Carnac, France. This is an area in Brittany, not far as the crow flies from Avebury. The huge stones of Carnac stretch for sometimes a mile over the landscape, in rows of ten, eleven or sometimes thirteen, until end-

The stones at Carnac

ing at their sacred destination. Here, as the scholar Rachel Levy says, is once again the old pathway, a "processional way greater than imagination" in which the stones themselves are considered divine.

The story of Joshua's march around the walls of Jericho (Joshua 6:1–21) is another example of a way. It is based, in all probability, on the custom of laying claim to territory by so tracing out its bounds. Gaster also tells us such circular marches were often part of the ceremonies at the installation of kings. In Egypt, for example, the new pharaoh circumambulated the fortified wall in a festal procession on the day of his enthronement. This ceremony was called "the circuit of the wall." More recently, in 1875, the new king of Thailand ritually circuited his palace and city at the time of his enthronement. In Britain, still in some places, there is an old custom called "beating the bounds." The local vicar marches around the confines of the parish in solemn procession; every so often a choirboy, or some other functionary, is lifted by his legs and his head "bumped" on the boundary line. Now that is a solemn ceremony I would like to see.

Another type of Way travels upward. You can see examples of this on many of the Chinese scrolls. These have always fascinated me, particularly the ones which have a painting of a person in the foreground, in front of a mountain, and winding around the mountain is a path that goes to the top. On the top of the mountain sits a shrine or a temple. In my mind, they are done in misty colors and they intrigue me with what feels like a great air of mystery and depth. Beverly Moon, in *An Encyclopedia of Archetypal Symbolism*, describes the journey up the sacred mountain, with its climb and accompanying rituals as a symbol of progress toward enlightenment.

A pilgrimage is another type of procession or way. It is a journey to the divine source, and usually includes such things as climbing a sacred mountain or the ritual of circumambulation. Islam has made the pilgrimage to Mecca called the Hajj, one of the cornerstones of the faith. Once there, according to Jill Purce who wrote *The Mystic Spiral*, the goal of the pilgrims' journey to Mecca is to achieve full understanding as he winds upward around the seven-fold path of the Ka'aba. which is the central shrine of Islam and Mecca. The center, the square stone of the Ka'aba, is the Temple of the Heart, and Islam's world axis. This ritual is so important that when the pilgrim returns he can proudly mark his house door to show he has made the pilgrimage.

According to Moon, the reason for the importance of this ritual is the meteorite called the Black Stone of Mecca, which is the Ka'aba, whose sacredness was due primarily to its heavenly origin. The Black Stone was sacred to the pre-Islamic Arabs long before the birth of Muhammad (c. 570 CE).

Barbara Walker, in the *Woman's Encyclopedia of Myths and Secrets*, tells us that originally, the Shrine of the sacred stone in Mecca was formerly dedicated to the pre-Islamic Triple Goddess Manat, Al-Lat, and Al-Uzza, who was the "Old Woman" worshipped by Muhammad's tribesmen the Koreshites. The stone was also called Kubaba, Kuba, or Kube, and has been linked with the name of Cybele, the Great Mother of the Gods. Esther Harding, in *Woman's Mysteries, Ancient & Modern*, tells us that on the stone is a yoni, which is a feminine symbol of the womb and the Great Goddess. The stone is covered with a black material called "the shirt of the Kaaba" and is served by men who are called *Beni Shaybah* which means the "Sons of the Old Woman."

Today, this traditionally feminine sacred spot is regarded as the holy center of patriarchal Islam, and its feminine symbolism has been lost. Yet the priests of the Ka'aba are still known as "Sons of the Old Woman." During the Prophet's lifetime, the Ka'aba was the principal religious shrine of central Arabia. Muhammad captured the shrine, removed all evidence of earlier deities, and dedicated it to the one God of his monotheistic faith. Since that time, the Ka'aba has been the central object of Islamic pilgrimage.

Another type of Way, which I think is the most exciting, is the labyrinth. The labyrinth is a symbolic pilgrimage, and is found in many sacred contexts from very ancient days to today. The labyrinth is also a spiral. Many of us use the word maze to describe it. But there is an important difference. Labyrinths have one well-defined path which leads into the center and back out again. There are no dead ends, no tricks. Mazes offer a choice of paths and entrances and exits. Mazes challenge the choice-making part of ourselves, while a labyrinth engages our intuitive side. Walking a labyrinth is a symbolic pilgrimage, and is found in many sacred contexts. It indicates a movement from what is outside and visible to what is inside and invisible, and then, offers the possibility of return. This journey may be regarded as a return to the womb, a descent into the underworld, or a journey to the center of the world. Walking the labyrinth is often connected to an initiation rite, one that seeks to bring about a spiritual transformation of the initiate. Labyrinths are still used as a spiritual tool. In the mail recently, I received a pamphlet advertising a series of religiously-oriented workshops. One was a retreat called "The Labyrinth: A Walking Meditation." Its description stated it "offers opportunities to traverse this mysterious winding path as a way to deepen our relationship with God and gain energy, vision, and clarity for our lives." Not much has changed over the years.

The most famous ancient labyrinth was the one on Crete, which, according to the old Greek myths, was home to the mythical halfman-halfbull called the Minotaur. He was killed by the Athenian hero, Theseus, with the help of Ariadne, a Cretan princess. Even though this wandering type of passage named by the myth gave the labyrinth its name, there are drawings of much older labyrinths found in the ancient world. Drawings of labyrinths even older than the Cretan one have been found in as diverse places as Ireland and Finland.

Purce reminds us that, in the physical movement of the turns and circles of certain dances—she mentions the Scottish dances—we are activating the inner energies and their cosmic counterparts in much the same way as walking the labyrinth. In Britain, there are still some historic turf mazes with Troy in their names. Even today elaborate processions and dances take place on some of them as a reminder of the "Easter Maze" dance occasions of the past. Children today play on a pattern of seven labyrinthine circles cut in the sod in a game called "Troy Town." Purce tells us that, by their spiral movements, they made chaos into cosmos, and protected the holy space they formed. The maze dance seems to have come very early to Britain from the Eastern Mediterranean. Ancient rough stone mazes of the same pattern as the English are found in Scandinavia and Northeastern Russia.

At Glastonbury, in the English West Country that is associated with King Arthur's Isle of Avalon, there is a sacred mountain, the Tor, whose path up the mountain is cut in the classical form of the labyrinth. Jean Shinoda Bolen, in *Crossing to Avalon*, says that the legends and artifacts indicate it originally was a pagan holy center sacred to the Great Goddess. At some point in the past, probably way before King Arthur's time, people shaped a path,

The Glastonbury Tor

which winds its way around and up the mountain. Its terraces form seven concentric rings that can be walked without too much difficulty. The final turn is hard to do; and Bolen tells us some feel the labyrinth enters the Tor itself at this point. There are many folk legends from the area which regard the Tor as a magic place with inward tunnels and great mysteries.

During the Middle Ages in Europe, labyrinths were frequently placed in the floors of churches. No one seems to be sure why. Some say Christ is found in the center of the labyrinth; others say it represents a pilgrimage to Jerusalem. Like labyrinths the world over, as the Jungians would say, its origin and motive are shrouded deep within the human psyche. Some powerful unconscious drive must be at work for humans to create the identical pattern in places as far separated in time and distance as, say, a rock at Tintagel, in the English West Country, a coin design from Crete, and an ancient symbol for the Earth Mother among the Hopi Indians of what is now Arizona.

The pagan tradition of walking the labyrinth as an initiation event was taken over by Christian authorities. The medieval cathedral of Chartes has a labyrinth in the floor of its nave with the six petaled rose of Aphrodite at its center. The path was exactly 666 feet long, which is Aphrodite's sacred number. According to Purce, in medieval cathedrals such as Chartres, there sometimes is a depiction of Theseus and the Minotaur. The symbolism is that of the "original" Cretan labyrinth—an initiatory hero test, the overcoming of death at the center, and a subsequent return or rebirth into life—a regeneration on a higher winding. For, just as it is necessary to be born from the womb to see this world, only he who is born from himself sees the other world. Other cathedral labyrinths depicted the architect at the center, sometimes symbolized in the person of Daedalus, builder of the Cretan maze. Since treading the maze was a pilgrimage to Jerusalem in miniature, Daedalus also represents the Divine architect. Such ritual walking of a pattern was said to represent a pilgrimage to the Holy Land and back again. The Chartres type of labyrinth, which is somewhat different than the basic maze, is found in manuscripts, church reliefs, mosaics, and English gardens. Usually it was circular, although occasionally it was octagonal. Then, by the pattern of its pathway, the circle of the labyrinth was divided into four quarters.

Rachel Levy tells us what is carried in the procession along the way is also very important. Frequently, it is the image of the deity, which seems to be a universal element of the ancient religions. Their purpose is to connect and to reinforce with the energy currents of the earth. A procession, interspersed with stations, traces the route of the currents and, by carrying an image or other object charged with spiritual power over the route, serves to fix and sanctify those items, and to benefit the people taking part in the rite. In medieval Christianity, the Corpus Christi Day procession was the principal ritual of this kind, in which the consecrated Host was carried around the town. The processions at coronations and the funeral cortege of a celebrity, still practiced today, serve similarly to distribute the virtue of the monarch or hero among his people. Roads taken by the divine power are the currents of energy. Examples of this are the Chinese dragons carried at the New Year Day parades to this day, or the Roman eagles in their parades (since a military march-past is a form of procession).

The idea of the Way is found all over the world. From China comes an ancient religious book whose title is *Tao Te Ching*, which means The Book (ching) of the Virtue or Power (te) of the Way (Tao). The word *Tao* means a road, path, way—the same as it does in the western culture. My editor tells me the way described in this ancient writing was one of inner growth.

For the most part, today we use the phrase "the way" to describe inner growth. For us, we use such expressions as "inner ways of development," or express ideas of "orientation" and "disorientation." We make references to philosophical, political, artistic "trends," when we want to talk about something intellectually or emotionally moving, which it is hoped, brings increased development. All of these related ideas are descended from what Neumann calls the "archetype of the way," which he sees as an originally unconscious pattern of humans moving toward a sacred goal. It keeps us out there, still moving.

FOR FURTHER READING

Bolen, Jean Shinoda. *Crossing to Avalon*. San Francisco: HarperSanFrancisco, 1994. Print.

Dames, Michael. *The Avebury Cycle*. London: Thames and Hudson Ltd., 1977. Print.

Campbell, Joseph. *Masks of God, Oriental Mythology*. New York: Penguin Books, 1976. Print.

Cirlot, J. E. *A Dictionary of Symbols*. New York: Philosophical Library, Inc., 1962. Print.

Gaster, Theodore, H. *Myth, Legend and Custom in the Old Testament*. New York: Harper Torchbooks, 1975. Print.

Godwin, Joscelyn. *Mystery Religions in the Ancient World*. San Francisco: Harper & Row, 1981. Print.

Hitching, Francis. *The Mysterious World, An Atlas of the Unexplained*. New York: Holt, Rinehart and Winston, 1979. Print.

Levy, Gertrude Rachel. *The Gate of Horn*. London: Faber & Faber, 1946. Print.

Michell, John. *The Earth Spirit: Its Ways, Shrines and Mysteries*. London: Thames and Hudson, 1975. Print.

Moon, Beverly, Ed. *An Encyclopedia of Archetypal Symbolism*. Boston: Shambala, 1991. Print.

Neumann, Erich. *The Great Mother*. Princeton, NJ: Princeton University Press, 1974. Print.

Osmen, Sarah Ann. *Sacred Places, A Journey into the Holiest Lands*. New York: St. Martin's Press, 1990. Print.

Purce, Jill. *The Mystic Spiral, Journey of the Soul*. London: Thames and Hudson, 1974. Print.

Sjoo, Monica, and Mor, Barbara. *The Great Cosmic Mother*. New York: Harper & Row, 1987. Print.

Streep, Peg. *Sanctuaries of the Goddess, The Sacred Landscapes and Objects*. Boston: Bulfinch Press Books, 1994. Print.

Walker, Barbara. *The Woman's Encyclopedia of Myths and Secrets*. San Francisco: HarperSanFrancisco, 1983. Print.

Wosein, Mariea-Gabriele. *Sacred Dance, Encounter with the Gods*. London: Thames and Hudson, 1992. Print.

CHAPTER 12

The Double Axe

AROUND HER NECK SHE WORE A SMALL GOLDEN DOUBLE axe, a labrys. It looked like a butterfly, or maybe two triangles whose points touch. I knew immediately from photographs and drawings, even though I had never seen one, she was wearing a labrys, the central symbol of the ancient goddess culture of Minoan Crete. When I asked my friend why she wore it, she replied it was her symbol of womanly courage. I nodded agreement, then asked where she found it. She answered Greece, which was puzzling. I forgot Crete today is part of Greece. When my friend added she got her labrys in Crete, I felt much better. I complimented her on her choice. The double axe is a perfect symbol for a woman; and Crete is exactly the right place to get one, because in ancient times the double axe was the basic symbol of the Goddess culture for Crete.

When most of us think of ancient Greece, we think of the historical period, the Greece of Socrates or Plato. Actually, in terms of the history of the world, that great period of Greece, around the fifth century BCE

(Before the Common Era), is really quite late. Scholars believe civilization as we know it, which means settled communities involved with agriculture, began after the ending of the last Ice Age, which was around 10,000 BCE, or 12,000 years or so ago. One author suggested our understanding of time would be a lot clearer if the dating of our calendar went back to the beginning of civilization, rather than picked it up in the middle. Anyway, these first civilizations in the ancient world developed a system of beliefs, traditions and law which focused on the female.

The deity for these societies was the Great Goddess. Her rituals dealt with the ongoing cycles of time, from birth to death to rebirth, again and again. Neolithic Europe worshipped a Mother Goddess, as did Libya and Syria. Norma Goodrich, in her book, *The Priestesses*, tells us that in Crete, the moon, especially, was revered in the form of the Triple Goddess, mistress of air, earth, and sea. The full moon represented the Goddess on earth and the first woman. She was "Queen of the Night."

Crete was one of the last strongholds of this ancient world. We don't know how it was destroyed. Anne Baring and Jules Cashford, in *The Myth of the Goddess*, tells us it happened around 1500 BCE, which is when the Indo-European invaders conquered the Goddess-worshipping communities around the Mediterranean. There doesn't seem to be evidence of an invasion. Possibly, the destruction came through earthquakes. Since it wasn't until the early part of the 20th century that the ruins of Crete were discovered and evacuated by Sir Arthur Evans, our surprise at what is there is relatively new. Evans called the culture of Crete "Minoan" after the King Minos found in Homer.

The story of Cretan civilization began around 8,000 years ago, when immigrants—probably from Anatolia (now Turkey)—first arrived. Monica Sjoo and Barbara Mor, in *The Great Cosmic Mother*, tell us they brought the Goddess with them as well as an agrarian technology. For the next four thousand years, there was slow and steady technological progress in pottery making, weaving, metallurgy, engraving, architecture and other crafts, as well as increasing trade, and the gradual evolution of a lively and joyful artistic style. Around 2000 BCE, Crete reached the peak of its development. This was already well into what we call the Bronze Age, which is when the rest of the civilized world was warlike and acquiring powerful male gods. Crete was the last full flowering of matriarchal culture.

The Great Goddess of Crete is a well-known figure. She stands, holding coiling snakes in her raised hands, barebreasted, dressed only in a flounced skirt. The wonderful skirt was worn also by both the Maltese and the Sumerian Goddess. In Crete, the uncovering of the breast was a sacred gesture, and part of the Minoan cult. The Goddess, and the priestesses identified with Her, showed their full breasts, symbols of the nourishing lifestream of the Mother. All of the widely distributed "Astarte"-type Great Goddesses, pressing or showing their breasts, have the same significance. In ancient days, milk was considered a miraculous gift of the female. The female deity was the source of nourishment and abundance. After I got into this symbol search, I realized being nursed was a means of empowerment, a symbolic expression for adoption by the Goddess. It is a very old idea, which goes back to before the days of the Pharaoh. When the Pharaoh sat on the lap on the goddess and nursed at her breast, he did this in order to receive the power from the Goddess, which gave him the right to rule. Whenever the worship of the Great Mother occurred, ritual emphasis was on the sacredness of life.

On the island of Crete when the Goddess still reigned, there are no signs of war. Marija Gimbutas, in *Civilization of the Goddess*, tells us that the economy prospered and the arts flourished. At the palace at Knossos, the capital of Crete, walls, ceilings and floors were often decorated with paintings. The subjects of these were usually sea and land plants, ritual activities and the life of the palace and people. Worship of nature was everywhere. No grand scenes of battle or hunting appear. In addition, to illustrate the comfort level of life, the Queen had her own bathroom with running water and something like a flush toilet. Personal ambition seems to have been unknown, even among the ruling classes. Nowhere do we find the name of an author attached to a work of art, or a record of the deeds of a ruler.

In the ruins, they found frescoes of beautiful, elegant women dressed in exquisite costumes. Barbara Walker, in *The Woman's Dictionary of Symbols & Sacred Objects*, says they are shown mixing freely with men in festivals, riding in chariots driven by female charioteers, and participating as athletes during the ritual bull games. Frescoes from Thera (an island just north of Crete, which was destroyed and abandoned by a massive earthquake) show women presiding at large naval festivals, standing on balconies, overseeing processions of young men who are carrying an animal for sacrifice. Walker tells us the seat of honor in the throne room at Knossos (the ancient capital of Crete) was most likely for the priestess who represented the Goddess. The throne was decorated with a circle and a crescent, and griffins (a composite mythological animal, which was a winged, eagle-headed, goat-bearded and lion-bodied) were painted on the wall on each side.

According to Gimbutas, men also appear in the art, but never as priests or kings and rarely, very rarely in images depicting a god. Men are usually shown engaged in occupations such as cup bearers, pages, musicians, harvesters, craftsmen and sailors. As for dress in the frescos, men who were old and of high status wore long robes; rustics wore fur or skin coats; young men participating in rituals are shown nude with hip belts.

As you might expect in a community which followed the Great Goddess, many of the social and political customs granted status to women. As we are told by Gimbutas, marriage in Crete was matrilocal, which means the couple lived with the female's family. This custom continued until late in the historical period. From discovered records, we know that a woman at marriage retained full control of her property and the right of divorce at her pleasure. Sounds good to me! In addition, the mother's brother had an important role and was responsible for bringing up her children.

The Minoan Cretans appear to have been gentle, joyous, sensuous and peace loving. From the evidence of ruins, they maintained at least 1,000 years of culture unbroken by war. The only other peoples we know of with such a long peaceful record were also Mother Goddess cultures. In Crete, for the last time in recorded history, a spirit of harmony between women and men as joyful and equal participants in life appears to pervade. According to Riane Eisler in *The Chalice and the Blade*, there seems to have been an equitable sharing of wealth. The general standard of living, judging from homes the archeologists have excavated, seems to have been high. There appears to have been institutionalized distribution of wealth throughout the community. They even had indoor plumbing. The public works include viaducts, paved roads, roadside shelters, fountains and reservoirs. The palaces in Crete had vast courtyards and hundreds of rooms. Eisler tells us gardens were an essential feature in Crete, as were buildings designed for privacy, good natural light and convenience.

The most famous and frequent symbol of Crete is the labrys, the double axe. The double triangle was widely used as a sign for woman. It is one of the emblems of the Goddess. It may have begun as a practical tool, but it became a religious symbol. The axe might be made in bronze of a gigantic size or very often in gold and be small. Sjoo and Mor tell us it was carried only by women. The palace of Knossos was known as The House of the Double Axes. As Jaquetta Hawkes states in her book *Dawn of the Gods*, in the palace and everywhere else the symbol was displayed as frequently as the cross is shown in Christian buildings.

The double axe is a very ancient symbol, and has been found in the Paleolithic caves of Niaux in southwest France from approximately 15,000 years ago. In Crete, the great bronze double-headed axes stood on shafts some six and a half feet high on either side of the altars of the goddess, where priestesses celebrating Her rites held them in their hands or on their heads. They also marked the entrances to Her sanctuaries. Baring and Cashford tell us that there are double axes patterned with roses or decorated with lilies. Both of these flowers have always been associated with the Great Goddess. Used in this way, the flowers evoke the presence of the Goddess in the same was that flowers today in Christian art evoke the presence of the Virgin Mary.

Baring and Cashford state that the two double axes held in the Goddess's hands may be understood as symbolizing Her rulership over the related domains of life and death. The sacred axe was the ritual instrument that sacrificed the bull, the cult animal that embodied the regenerative power of the Goddess. The double axe was also used to cut down the tree which was probably an annual ceremony. In Crete, the tree was worshipped as the image of the Goddess herself, and a special ritual and a sacred axe were required when a tree was cut down. Since the axe never appears in Crete held by a man or male priest, it does not seem to carry the later Aryan association of the axe with The God of Thunder.

Archeologist Marija Gimbutas, in *The Language of the Goddess*, sees the double axe as a butterfly. Butterflies have been found on artifacts from before humans learned to shape metal axes, several thousand years before this time. Therefore, she says the axes from the second millennium BCE copied the image of the butterfly. Both the axe and the butterfly are associated with the Great Goddess. Gimbutas states the idea of a double axe, which is hourglass shaped, came from the hourglass-shaped Goddess of Death and Regeneration. To the ancients, the life cycle of the caterpillar, chrysalis and butterfly was a powerful symbol of life, death and resurrection. In antiquity, the image of a butterfly emerging from the chrysalis stood for the soul leaving the body at death. It is a particularly good example to show the movement of cyclic time, or the transformations in life, as the butterfly is a species where something changes from one thing (a chrysalis) to another thing (the butterfly). In very early days Gimbutas suggests the caterpillar and the butterfly together were two aspects in a single life form; one was "born" out of the other. The double axe is the symbol of rebirth in the form of a butterfly. The butterfly in many lands is still an image of the soul. In Greek, the word for butterfly and soul is the same, "psyche." In both Western Europe and the Far East, the butterfly was considered a soul symbol. The idea was that human souls became butterflies while searching for a new reincarnation.

To equate the labrys with the butterfly symbol makes it consistent with the image of the Great Goddess as the ongoing and never-ending cycle of time from birth to death to rebirth. Agricultural societies see vegetation grow, die and then rise again the following year. This creates a vision of life and death experienced as one sacred whole. Whenever the Great Goddess was worshipped, her rituals emphasized the sacredness of this unity.

I was reminded of the ancient symbolism of butterflies when I visited the National Holocaust Museum in Washington. They built there a long wall, which is decorated with individual tiles painted by children from all over the country. The heading over the wall was titled something like "from the children will come rebirth." Each of the tiles is a child's expression of the horror of the Holocaust. There are of course quite a few six pointed Stars of David, swastikas facing both left and right and tiles displaying butterflies. Some of the butterflies were even in the ancient double axe shape of touching triangles. Even though I knew the butterflies related to the children's poem "I Never Saw Another Butterfly" from Hitler's model Terezin concentration camp, I found it very moving; and somehow it felt very right.

The word labyrinth, of course, is connected to the labrys. It means "House of the Double Axe," the name given to the palace at Knossos. It, more than any of the other palaces of Crete, had large open courtyards and hundreds of rooms arranged in no particular pattern or style. Ritual processions, which moved through these rooms and courtyards, went from light to dark to light again. In the cave-like center of the palace there was the shrine marked with double axes. There the Goddess, or her priestess acting in her place, probably sat on Her throne. Scholars today feel it was this palace itself that was the famous Labyrinth of Greek mythology.

A Labyrinth is a spiral. It is a design which created a journey into the other world and out again. Walking a labyrinth, according to Mircea Eliade in *A History of Religious Ideas*, was the equivalent to a descent into Hades. In other words, it is equivalent to a ritual death of the initiatory type. It was like all the sacred cyclic journeys of death and rebirth. Getting lost was not the idea of a classic labyrinth, as it had only one path which went into all parts of the figure. The journey into the central chamber seems to have been a rebirth ritual. This pilgrimage, of course, is a ritual consistent with the birth to death to rebirth idea expressed in the labrys and the butterfly.

One of the main rituals of the Minoan Cretans was the walking or dancing of the labyrinth. The Minoan Cretans felt one could approach the divine by physically walking such a labyrinth. Doing so permitted them to participate in a journey to the other world. This idea was prevalent in the ancient world. As Elinor Gadon tells us in *The Once and Future Goddess*, Crete, as well as the present day Hopi Indians in the American Southwest, both depict the maze (a labyrinth is a type of maze) as the mythic place of place of birth, or rebirth. The Hopi Indians see the labyrinth as similar to the Kiva, their underground sanctuary, out of which the Hopi people came into the world.

Sjoo and Mor state that extremely complex ideas were expressed through the symbol of the labyrinth.

> First, the initiate had to find the way through the underworld—the womb of the Mother—going through symbolic death to be reborn through her on a larger psychic level. Simultaneously, by dancing the winding and unwinding spiral, the initiate reached back to the still heart of the cosmos, and so to immortality, in Her. The dance would have been combined with sexual rites and the taking of some hallucinogen like the legendary soma. In the resulting illumination soma and self were experienced as one with the cosmic self in orgasmic ego-death.

While the winding, ritual way at Knossos may have given the concept of a labyrinth, its name, the symbol of the winding spiral is much older. We do not know what the labyrinth at Knossos looked like. Francis Hitching, in *The Mysterious World*, tells us we do have Cretan coins from a later period that are engraved with a basic spiral labyrinth. Its clearly-defined convoluted spiral pathway goes to and from the center. The spiral type of maze, however, is the most commonly shaped labyrinth, and one which besides being found in Crete, has been found in all parts of the world.

The myth which made the Labyrinth at Knossos in Crete famous is, of course, the legend of Theseus and the Minotaur. According to the myth, which is only a piece of a longer story, at the center of the Labyrinth lived the fearsome Minotaur—half man, half bull. Every nine years, the Athenians were bound to sacrifice seven young boys and seven maidens to him. Daedalus, the architect of the maze, designed it with so many clever twists and turns and false exits that the victims would lose their way, and so were slaughtered by the Minotaur. Theseus was a young Athenian hero who offered himself as one of the fourteen. When he arrived in Crete, Ariadne, the daughter of the King of Crete, fell in love with him. She gave him a ball of thread to re-trace his steps through the Labyrinth. In this way, he was able to slay the Minotaur and lead his group to safety. As told by Greek legend, this is a tale of a hero vanquishing a monster and freeing his country from a cruel oppression.

However, the Minoan Cretans tell a different story. Theseus's victory in the center of the Labyrinth, which they considered the body of the Goddess, was the deathblow to the way of the Goddess. After that, the Labyrinth was transformed into the dreaded kingdom of the dead, without the concept of death being viewed as rebirth in the body of the Mother. All the Greek myths show a revision of this type, which was necessary to adapt the Goddess-oriented myths to the god-oriented culture of the conquering community.

What Crete, through the labrys and the labyrinth left us, then, is a vision which experiences life and death as one sacred whole. Can it be a coincidence that for thousands of years the people of Crete lived, not only in harmony with the rhythms of nature, which they experienced as a Great Goddess, but also lived in peace? No wonder my friend wears a labrys around her neck.

FOR FURTHER READING

Baring, Anne, and Cashford, Jules. *The Myth of the Goddess*. London: Viking/Arkana 1991. Print.
Eisler, Riane. *The Chalice and the Blade*. New York: Harper & Row, 1988. Print.
Gadon, Elinor W. *The Once & Future Goddess*. New York: HarperCollins, 1989. Print.
Green, Peter. *Ancient Greece, An Illustrated History*. London: Thames & Hudson, 1973. Print.

Gimbutas, Marija. *Civilization of the Goddess.* New York: Harper, 1991. Print.

———. *The Goddesses and Gods of Old Europe.* Berkeley: University of California Press, 1982. Print.

———. *The Language of the Goddess.* New York: Harper & Row, 1989. Print.

Goodrich, Norma Lorre. *The Priestesses.* New York: HarperCollins, 1989. Print.

Grant, Michael. *The Ancient Mediterranean.* New York: Penguin Books, 1988. Print.

Graves, Robert. *The Greek Myths, Vol. 1.* New York: Viking Penguin, 1955. Print.

———. *The White Goddess.* New York: HarperCollins, 1966. Print.

Hall, James. *Dictionary of Subjects & Symbols in Art.* New York: Harper & Row, 1979. Print.

Harrison, Jane. *Prolegomena to the Study of Greek Religion.* Princeton, NJ: Princeton University Press, 1991. Print.

Hawkes, Jaquetta. *Dawn of the Gods.* New York: Random House, 1968. Print.

Hitching, Frances. *The Mysterious World, An Atlas of the Unexplained.* New York: Rinehart & Winston, 1979. Print.

Levy, Gertrude Rachel. *The Gate of Horn.* London: Faber & Faber, 1948. Print.

Moon, Beverly, Ed. *An Encyclopedia of Archetypal Symbolism.* Boston: Shambala, 1991. Print.

Neumann, Erich. *The Great Mother.* Princeton, NJ: Princeton University Press, 1974. Print.

CHAPTER 13

Blood and Sacrifice

WHILE WANDERING THROUGH THE BRITISH MUSEUM IN London, I found what British schoolchildren call "The Peat Marsh Man," the remains of a male body found in a peat bog. According to the Museum, he was put in the bog sometime between 300 BCE (Before the Common Era) and 100 CE (Common Era). His death had not been an easy one. He had suffered what Robert Graves, in *The Greek Myths*, called the ritual three times murder; first being hit on the head, second being garroted with a thin cord, and third, having his throat cut. Obviously, this was not a casual event. According to the Museum, such a death indicates a ritual killing, a human sacrifice. The obvious question is "why?"

Archeologists tell us that human sacrifice is very old. It took place all through the early Neolithic (Stone Age) communities, and as the existence of Peat Marsh Man tells us was still being done in England as late as 300 to 100 BCE. According to Nigel Davies in *Human Sacrifice in History and Today*, human sacrifice in one form or another took place all over the ancient Near East as well as China. To an uncanny degree both places use the same patterns of practice. No matter the location, for sacrificial purposes each community seemed to have shared the same goals and chose similar types of victims. Then we are told by

133

Patrick Tierney in *The Highest Altar, The Story of Human Sacrifice*, that today in the Andes it still occurs, although no one there talks about it.

The word "sacrifice" comes from the Latin *sacer facere*, "to make whole or sacred." This has the sense of restoring to wholeness something which has been lost. Davies describes the act of sacrifice as an important rite which reunites the community and restores its equilibrium. Tierney tells us that human sacrificial myth and ritual were behind many of the ancient celebrations. He says it was the force behind such rituals as the "Panhellenic celebrations at Mount Olympus, Bronze Age ceremonies at Stonehenge, Jewish holidays at the Great Temple on Mount Moriah and dynastic offerings atop the Mayan pyramids."

Davies describes the purpose of the sacrifice in this way: "In essence human sacrifice was an act of piety. Both sacrificer and victim knew that the act was required, to save the people from calamity, and the cosmos from collapse." As Monica Sjoo and Barbara Mor, in *The Great Cosmic Mother*, put it, the ancients realized they were able to live only by eating other living things, both animal and vegetable. This created a situation for them that could only be resolved by creating rituals to deal with the guilt of the killing.

The reason the ancients felt guilty is they believed the earth was the body of the Great Mother Goddess. Believing this meant normal agricultural functions, such as plowing or picking crops, felt like "killing" or "eating" Mother Earth. Such "crimes" created a deep need to atone; and human sacrifice became the vehicle to make things right. To us, this feels like a strange type of reasoning. To the ancients, the ritual was central to their religious activities. In the earliest times, the gory fragments of the sacrificial victim were handed round as precious gifts and offered up to the "earth" to help bring forth greater fertility from the "earth." Anne Baring and Jules Cashford, in *The Myth of the Goddess*, say that "In the ritual of sacrifice human beings project and focus their fear of death on a specific human or animal, so that the slaying of this particular living being is at the same time a slaying of their fear, for the death of the other substitutes for their own."

As Sjoo and Mor tell us, during the Stone Age, during the time of worship of the Great Mother, ritual community sacrifices were a mixture of blood sacrifices and sexual rites, combined with mourning the dead, ploughing the fields, and harvesting crops. All this was done in the belief that the mingling of blood and semen would renew the Great Mother, which would help the seeds to grow and the dead to be reborn. The ancients felt these group sexual activities were important and necessary religious rituals to encourage the deity to keep the world in balance.

Early sacrifices were very bloody affairs. Erich Neumann, in *The Great Mother*, tells us blood was very important. Blood is life; shedding blood is loss of life, and death. This is why the shedding of blood was a sacred act, whether it was the blood of a wild beast, a domestic animal, or a man. In New Stone Age times people believed it was the blood of the sacrificed victim soaking into the ground which fertilized the ground and made the crops grow. Baring and Cashford tell us that the renewal of life was associated with the shedding of blood as far back as the Paleolithic, the Old Stone Age, times, when red-ochre covered the bodies for burial as a substitute for blood. This was done because blood was regarded as the life-force itself.

While blood was widely prohibited as a food, sometimes during ceremonies the ancients drank it to absorb the life-force and power of a slain enemy. Mingling of blood was also used in rites of atonement, to seal covenants, and to establish kinship or friendship. We still see this old idea in the Cowboy and Indian movies when they become "Blood Brothers" by mixing their blood. Or, as Barbara Walker, in *The Women's Dictionary of Symbols & Sacred Objects*, tells us, "When two drank together from the cup offered to heaven, they became as one blood in the sight of God." This idea became part of the pagan marriage ceremony. The aim was to make bride and groom one blood in the eyes of the god. Blood smeared on doorposts or used for writing also had magical qualities.

Of course, to the ancients, the menstrual blood of women was the tie between humans and the Great Mother. This connection became one of the underlying ideas in the worship of the Great Mother. Ancient communities saw the blood of menstruation, defloration, and birth as natural connections to the magical world.

Baring and Cashford tell us that blood is always associated with the Goddess. She has the blood magic that makes life grow. She can take her blood and turns it into a baby. Her rites were bloody, Her festivals sexual. Neumann tells us, "The womb of the earth clamors for fertilization, and blood sacrifices and corpses are the food she likes best." In all the places where the Great Mother was worshiped, She always was regarded as the Goddess of the hunt and of war. This is the dark side of worship of the Great Mother, a side which cannot be forgotten nor ignored; and it is the side that demands blood sacrifices. All the ancient people of the world combined the birth-life-and death-giving powers of earth to the Mother Goddess. Neumann states the Great Goddess was not only the nourishing Goddess who gives and sustains life, but also the Goddess of savagery, bloodlust, and destruction.

The world of the Great Mother was shaped by cycles. The ancients may have developed this concept from watching the cycles of the phases of the moon. Each month the moon starts very small, becomes full, and then shrinks until it disappears for three nights of total darkness. They saw a connection between the cycles of the moon and the cycles of life. To the ancients, the main cycle of life was the birth-life-death cycle. The three days of the dark time of the moon cycle was felt to be the time of death. It was an important time because here is where the next cycle begins. Death, to the ancients, was the first step to rebirth.

During the three days of darkness of the moon, the Dark Goddess aspect of the Great Goddess ruled. As Demetra George in *Mysteries of the Dark Moon* says, during this time the ancients saw the dark of the moon as a symbol of the awesome underworld. Also these two to three nights of darkness frequently were the time of menstruation for the women of the community. (Studies have shown that women who live together tend to menstruate together, and that women are most likely to menstruate at the dark of the moon or at the full moon.) This was a time of terrible power.

The ancients saw the moon as weakened and devoured by the powers of darkness during its waning phases. Sjoo and Mor say that the Goddess, in her death aspect, is the earth in which things rot. She was the ruler of death and the underworld. The role of the Dark Goddess was to receive the dead and prepare them for rebirth. She had the wisdom that came from experience, and because of this she ruled over winter, the underworld, magical arts, secret knowledge, and oracles. In the art from that time she has the fearful face of the goddess who devours life. In some figures she is an old woman showing her vulva which symbolized renewal.

The Dark Goddess was known by many names. As George lists them these are only a few of the ones I recognized: Kali from India, Hekate and Persephone from Greece, Lilith from the Near East, Morgana from Britain, and Hel from Scandinavia. Other personifications of Her are the Fates, the Furies, Medusa, Medea, Circe, the Gorgons, the Sirens, the Black Madonna, Cerrwiden, Black Isis, Oya, Mother Holle, Baba Yaga, the Terrible Mother, the Bad Fairy and the Wicked Witch. This list is far from complete. All of these are strong female figures who represented the powerful forces of the dark of the moon—death, sex, power. While in many legends these females are old and ugly, in others they are youngish, sexy and beautiful. Always they are powerful, fearful, and when treated with respect, helpful. Within the Great Goddess communities they received awe, reverence and respect. The Jungians would say they represent the strong forces, many of which are destructive, within each of us. These are the powers which can be used for healing and for new growth. The current idea that sees growth coming from destruction would be quite comfortable in the ancient world.

Fertilizing the earth was the reason for the necessity of sacrifice. According to Walker, human or animal, the sacrificial victims of ancient cultures were almost invariably male. Therefore, male blood only was poured out on the earliest altars, in imitation of the female blood that gave "life." Legends consistently associate kingship with ceremonial death. The belief was that kings possessed magical or supernatural powers by virtue of which they can fertilize the earth. This idea seems to have been shared, according to Sir James George Frazer in *The Golden Bough*, by the ancestors of all the Aryan races from India to Ireland. Neumann assures us that in ancient time a human victim, whether god, king, or priest, was always offered up to ensure the fertility of the earth.

It seems, according to Robert Graves in *The Greek Myths*, that each year the queen/priestess of the Goddess chose a young lover to be king. He was then sacrificed at the end of that year. This made him a symbol of fertility, rather than the object of erotic pleasure. His sprinkled blood served to fructify trees, crops, and flocks, and his flesh was torn and eaten raw by the queen's fellow priestesses. The consort of the queen/priestess acquired executive power only when permitted to deputize for the queen by wearing her magical robes. Thus kingship developed.

From the earliest days, according to Esther Harding in *Woman's Mysteries, Ancient and Modern*, we find evidence of a Great Mother Goddess reigning supreme with Her son/lover. Her choice depended largely on the candidate's sex appeal. Sexual potency was an important job qualification for these young consorts. A common method to test his virility was to have him look on the naked Goddess as She annually restored Her virginity by taking a magical ritual bath. Some of the old legends suggest that the king was selected by the promptness of his erection. Walker tells us that Bath-Sheba, whose name meant she was the daughter of Arabian queens, married King David after he saw her naked in her bath, and after he killed her previous husband, Uriah the Hittite (II Samuel 11).

Walker states that, if the Queen tired of the king's lovemaking, he could be deposed or killed, for the queen's sexual acceptance of him determined the fertility of the land. In many early societies, the old king was killed by the new king, usually called a "son" though he was no blood relative.

The ritual in which the king became a king took place when he married the priestess of the Goddess in a sacred marriage called the *hieros gamos*, an extremely important ritual in the ancient world. This sacred marriage was important since it was through this ceremony the goddess chose the candidate for kingship and then for sacrifice. Numerous accounts from ancient days tell of this sacred marriage between the priestess acting as goddess, and her consort. It was by the *hieros gamos*, that the consort received his power to be not only the king but also the god. This is the ritual that was the "holy matrimony." It was the essential act to create a king. In 1990, when the Japanese emperor became the emperor, a sacred marriage type of ceremony with the Rice Goddess was an essential part of the ritual. It was through this ceremony with the Rice Goddess that he became not only the emperor, but also a god. In today's world such a ceremony was quite controversial and everyone tried to downplay it, but there it was. Only by including this ritual in the coronation ceremonies would the emperor be acceptable to many Japanese.

According to Neumann, these youths whom the priestess chose were designated as vegetation deities. Not only were they fertility deities, but they also were considered the vegetation itself. "By their existence the earth is fruitful, but as soon as they reach maturity they must be killed, to be harvested. The youths who belong to the Great Mother are gods of spring who must be put to death in order to be lamented by the Great Mother and reborn." I know it sounds strange, but that's the way ancient communities constructed it. All lovers of Mother Goddesses were beautiful and pleased the amorous priestess/Goddesses by their physical beauty. We know of many of these "son-lovers" through the legends which have come down to us. In different languages, this youth has different names. Some of the names from the legends are Tammuz, Attis, Adonis, Osiris or Baal. These "son-lovers" always died young, which caused among those who honored the Goddess an annual period of grief and lamentation. Throughout the world, those communities which honored the Goddess shared similar legends and lamentation rituals. Walker also tells us that, in the ancient Middle East, kings were not so much governing figures as ceremonial ones. They were primarily concerned with the dedication of temples and other religious responsibilities.

According to Frazer, the belief that kings possess magical or supernatural powers by virtue of which they can fertilize the earth and confer other benefits on their subjects seems to have been shared by all of the Aryan races from India to Ireland, and it left traces of itself all through history down to modern times. In Homeric Greece, kings and chiefs were spoken of as sacred or divine. It was thought that the reign of a good king caused the black earth to bring forth wheat and barley, the trees to be loaded with fruit, the flocks to multiply, and the sea to yield fish. The ancients believed their safety, and even that of the world, was connected to the life of their god-like kings.

Being human, the kings tried to avoid being sacrificed. One way out was to be a war leader and be able to convince the people that no one else could defeat the enemy. In that case, a surrogate for the sacrifice had to be found. A popular surrogate was the king's son. Son-killing was routine. Stories of sons being sacrificed abound throughout the world. An example is the Swedish king named Aun who managed to extend his reign for nine years by each year sacrificing one of his ten sons to ransom his own life.

Robert Graves lists the various ritual ways to kill the king. He might be torn into pieces by wild women, transfixed with a sting-ray spear, felled with a axe, pricked in the heel with a poisoned arrow, flung over a cliff, burned to death on a pyre, drowned in a pool, or killed in a pre-arranged chariot crash. But die he must. When I read the list I kept thinking of all the old legends and stories that use these types of executions in their plots. According to Graves, such stories are tales whose roots come from this earliest period.

At some point, probably a king's idea after he acquired more real power, it was decided to extend the one year reign to a Great Year of 100 lunar months which is approximately eight plus years. Why a reign of eight years? The answer is probably found in astronomy. The ancient world marked rituals by the cycles of the moon. Solar time however, marked the seasons. The two cycles don't mesh easily. For example, only once in every eight years is the full moon on the same night as the longest or shortest day. To the ancients, meshing these two cycles was a matter of great concern, since the right time for some rituals was found in the lunar cycle and the right time for others was in the solar cycle. No wonder that it seemed a good idea that the death of the king, who also was the chief priest of the state and, by his connection to the priestess/goddess, also was a god, should come at a time when the two cycles coincided. But since the fields and crops still needed to be nourished annually, the king agreed each year that he would suffer a mock death. At this time, for a day, he gave up the kingship to a boy-king who was then killed in his place, so there would be blood for the sprinkling ceremony.

This belief, of connecting the community's health to a human king, presented a real problem since all men, even man-gods grow old and feeble. The ancient communities dealt with this danger by killing the man-god as soon as he showed symptoms of failing powers. They believed by doing this they would transfer his soul to a vigorous successor before his power was seriously reduced. By this action, they felt they preserved the safety of the community.

There were rituals in many of the ancient communities that reflected the relation between the king and the queen. Walker tells us that the ancient Romans killed their kings in a strange ceremonial ritual. Their kings usually were killed by "assassination" at the beginning of the sacred year which began in March. Remember Julius Caesar? He was killed at the fatal time, the Ides of March, in the sacred inner chamber of the senate, on the very dais of the altar.

Walker continues the story. In England, many of the tribes had relations between the king and the queen that reflect back to the days of the Goddess. Many of the pre-Christian British kings became kings through *hieros gamos* with the queen. The Pictish kings from Scotland were selected by the royal women from a matrilineal bloodline. Early Saxon queens governed their land, and a king could govern only by marrying them. Early British tales show the kings were only able to rule when they possessed the queen, whose name was Guinevere—also called Cunneware, Gwenhwyfar, Jennifer, Ginevra, or Genevieve. In the King Arthur stories, Guinevere constantly was involved with other men. By the interpretation here, she was the representation of the Mother Goddess and these men were would-be kings claiming to be her consort. It was not Guinevere being an ordinary adulteress. With this interpretation, I feel better about Guinevere. What seemed to be her lack of morals and discretion always disturbed me. In pagan Ireland, the king's inaugural greeting announced that he was wedded to (literally, had copulated with) his land, who was represented by the queen. This states the old idea of the land being the Goddess and the queen the representative of the Goddess.

The symbolism of the Goddesses' yearly youthful consorts, the dying son/lover of the Goddess, occurs and recurs throughout the legends of the Goddess religion, probably recording Neolithic and earliest historic periods. It is found in the most ancient legends of both Sumer and Egypt and survives in all historic periods of the Near East until the first centuries of Christianity, in which it may have been retained in the annual mourning for the death of Jesus.

Numerous accounts, legends and fragments of texts and prayers suggest that there were similar practices in most of the Goddess-worshiping cultures throughout the Near East, slightly different adaptations depending on the location and the gradual transitions that took place over the years. It does seem reasonable, then, to assume that the Peat Moss Man I found in the British Museum was most likely a consort who was sacrificed for the benefit of his community.

FOR FURTHER READING

Ackerman, Susan. "Sacred Sex, Sacrifice and Death." *Bible Review* 6, 8–44. February, 1990. Print.

Baring, Anne, and Cashford, Jules. *The Myth of the Goddess*. New York: Penguin, 1991. Print.

Cooper, J. C. *The Aquarian Dictionary of Festivals*. Wellingborough, Northamptonshire, England: The Aquarian Press, 1990. Print.

Davies, Nigel. *Human Sacrifice in History and Today*. New York: William Morrow & Co., 1982. Print.

Frazer, Sir James George. *The Golden Bough*. New York: Macmillan Publishing Co., 1922. Print.

Gadon, Elinor W. *The Once and Future Goddess*. New York: HarperCollins, 1989. Print.

George, Demetra. *Mysteries of the Dark Moon*. San Francisco: HarperSanFrancisco, 1992. Print.

Graves, Robert. *The Greek Myths, Vol. 1*. New York: Viking Penguin, 1955. Print.

Levy, Gertrude Rachel. *The Gate of Horn*. London: Faber & Faber, 1946. Print.

Moon, Beverly, Ed. *An Encyclopedia of Archetypal Symbolism*. Boston: Shambala, 1991. Print.

Neumann, Erich. *The Great Mother*. Princeton, NJ: Princeton University Press, 1963. Print.

———. *The History of Consciousness*. Princeton, NJ: Princeton University Press, 1970. Print.

Sjoo, Monica, and Mor, Barbara. *The Great Cosmic Mother*. New York: Harper & Row, 1987. Print.

Stone, Merlin. *When God Was a Woman*. New York: Harcourt Brace Jovanovich, 1976. Print.

Tierney, Patrick. *The Highest Altar, The Story of Human Sacrifice*. New York: Viking Penquin, 1989. Print.

Walker, Barbara. *The Woman's Dictionary of Symbols & Sacred Objects*. San Francisco: HarperSanFrancisco, 1988. Print.

CHAPTER 14

Rebirth of the Sun

IT WAS CHRISTMAS EVE. AS WE SAID GOOD-BYE, THE Buddhist shopkeeper and I, the Jewish customer, each wished the other a "Merry Christmas." As I walked out of the store, I thought, "This is crazy, why do we do this? This is not a holiday for either of us. While a lot of reasons popped into my head, the one that stuck was acknowledgment that even though neither of us was involved with the religious aspects of Christmas, the atmosphere of the time of the year—the lights, the music, the upbeat mood—make even non-participants like us respond to the festivities.

I remember the show I saw some years ago at the Planetarium. I was really pleased and surprised to see the usual December show had changed from the traditional three Magi's following the star to Bethlehem to a celebration of the Winter Solstice. With the story of the solstice came an explanation of how all the winter holidays through time developed from solstice celebrations of some sort.

We moderns are very much out of touch with how the changes of the seasons affect us. We also don't pay much attention to the seasonal events themselves. We think of the winter solstice as merely being the shortest day of the year and the first day of winter. It comes and it goes, and that is the end of it. We attach no drama, no mystery, no major religious significance to the event. Ancient communities were far more involved. While they didn't know why these things happened, which made the events very mysterious, they certainly knew something very important was taking place. Not only did they mark the shortening of the days, but they also noted the weakening of the sun's strength, which comes when the sun's path is lower in the sky. The only time in my life I really had to cope with this phenomenon was during the years I carpooled children to their various after school activities. I found the most depressing season was from late November through middle January. This was the period when the darkness descended earlier and earlier, an event that made the carpooling feel even more onerous. By mid-January, I became aware of the lengthening of the days, and my spirits always got a boost. Then even carpooling became less of a chore.

 Ancient communities, however, closely followed the yearly cycle of the sun. Since they had little knowledge of the science of what was happening, all they could do was observe the cycle and create all sorts of fantasy to explain it. E. O. James, in *Prehistoric Religion*, tells us that according to the ancient world in Mesopotamia, Anatolia, Syria and Greece, the first part of winter, from November through mid-December, was thought of as the yearly dying of the sun. These communities worshipped a vegetation year-god who died to be reborn as the child of the Great Goddess, the source of all life. They believed that, on the day of the winter solstice, the traditional divine child, who represented the birth of the sun, was born. Today, we know the winter solstice is the time of the year when sunrise takes place at the most southern point of the sun's yearly cycle through the sky. The sun hangs there for a few days, which is why it is called "solstice" (sun stand still). Then it begins its northern circuit of the sky until, six months later in late June, the sun rises at the most northern point of the yearly cycle, which is the summer solstice.

Now, if the cold facts of this don't sound very exciting, think of it this way: There you are, an ancient in a world of no artificial light or heat except a fire and maybe some torches or candles. Every morning when you awake before dawn, you see the sun rising over the distant mountains just a bit farther south than the day before. You know from past experience that it never goes farther south than let's say, the waterfall on a distant mountainside. You also know that, each day as the sun rises farther south, winter takes a stronger hold. It becomes colder and the days are shorter. Finally, the sun reaches the waterfall. You know that, if for some reason, this year the sun doesn't stop its moving at the waterfall but continues south past it, the world as you know it is finished. Winter will never end, and darkness and cold will take over the world. But, as always, the dawn comes when the sun not only stops, but starts heading back north. Now you know winter will end, the days will get longer, and all is right with the world. We are talking of a very serious event here, and from the beginning of civilization humans so marked it. Traditionally, this is the time of the year when the world was renewed, which means it is regarded as a new beginning and a new creation. It was also the time of the year for rededication and affirmation of faith. You get the full nine yards and a great party to boot.

By the calendar we use today, the winter solstice is the first day of winter. However, according to the ancient Celtic calendar, the solstice took place at mid-winter and winter started on November 1. The Celts divided the calendar year differently than we do. According to Robert Graves in *The Greek Myths*, the Celtic calendar in ancient times divided the year into thirteen months, each month having 28 days. There was an extra day which was put in the yearly cycle between the thirteenth month and the first month. We still carry the old calendar in our language in the expression "a year and a day." The extra day was the day of the winter solstice.

Demetra George, in *Mysteries of the Dark Moon*, tells us that, at the time of the winter solstice, the moon is full and high in the sky, the sun is at its lowest point. In the earliest mythologies night was given precedence over day and the moon precedence over the sun. Ancient communities thought all life came from the moon, which is why they considered the moon more important than the sun. Looked at this way, it becomes easy to understand how the idea of the moon giving birth to the sun developed. It then becomes easy to see how the imagery of the moon giving birth to the sun developed into the idea of the Virgin Goddess giving birth to a son—the divine Child—at the winter solstice. According to Erich Neumann in the *The Great Mother*, the idea that the winter solstice was the time when the Great Mother gave birth to the sun is at the center of the matriarchal mysteries.

> All over the world, for countless millennia, people have participated in a religious ritual at the winter solstice. These divine sons were born at midnight, hidden in the depths of the earth, in reeds, in a cave, out of a rock, in a manger. In Mesopotamia he was called Tammuz and Dumuzi; in Egypt he was called Osiris and Horus, and later, Aion; in Greece, Dionysos, Helios and Orpheus; in Persia and Rome, Mithras.

According to Sir James Frazer, in his classic *The Golden Bough*, the ancient Syrian and Egyptian ritual of the birth at the winter solstice was the following:

> The celebrants retired into certain inner shrines, from which at midnight they issued with a loud cry "The Virgin has brought forth. The light is waxing!" The Egyptians even represented the new-born sun by the image of an infant which on his birth-

day, the winter solstice, they brought forth and exhibited to his worshippers.

The priestesses who served the Great Goddess at the moon shrines and sanctuaries throughout the ancient Mediterranean world were called virgins. According to Sjoo and Mor in *The Great Cosmic Mother*, "Virgin" meant not married, not belonging to a man, a woman who was "one-in herself." The word derives from a Latin root meaning strength, force, skill. This is the same root used for the word virile to describe strong men. All the early Goddesses, Ishtar, Diana, Astarte, Isis were called virgin. This term did not refer to their sexual chastity, but to their sexual independence. In addition, all the great cultural heroes of the past, mythic or historic—Marduk, Gilgamesh, Buddha, Osiris, Dionysus, Ghengis Khan, Jesus—were said to be born of virgin mothers. When the Hebrews used the word, and in the original Aramaic, it meant "maiden" or "young woman," with no connotations of sexual chastity.

I was talking to my family about this imagery when my husband asked, "Why is the moon thought to be a woman?" I asked the young woman with us what 28 meant to her. After a few seconds she answered, "Either a month or a menstrual period." Jokingly, my husband said, "You mean the moon has a menstrual period." Actually, it works the other way. Women's menstrual periods follow the cycle of the moon, which is what made the ancients consider women to be agents of the life-giving moon who is personified as the Great Goddess. Both words "menses" and "month" are derived from the word "moon."

Joseph Campbell, in *Mythic Image*, says the Church seems to have borrowed the date of the festival of Christmas from the Persian Mithraic religion. Mithra was the Persian savior god who was the incarnation of eternal light. He was born at midnight at the time of the winter solstice. Under the calendar used at that time the date was December 25. The Gospels say nothing as to the day of Christ's birth and, accordingly, the early Church did not celebrate it. For the first three centuries of Christian life, the Christian church knew no birthday for its savior. During the fourth century, there was much argument about the adoption of a date. Some favored the popular date of the Koreion, which was when in Egyptian Alexandria, the divine Virgin gave birth to the new Aion. This date is now called Twelfth Night or Epiphany and is still the official Armenian nativity. The Roman church, though, favored the Mithraic winter-solstice festival. This December 25 nativity also honored such gods as Attis, Dionysus, Osiris, Syrian Baal, and other versions of the solar god. Most pagan mystery religions celebrated the birth of the Divine Child at the winter solstice. Norsemen celebrated the birthday of the Lord, Frey, in the darkest days of the winter, a time known to them as Yule. All of this made the choice of December 25 easy, as the people were used to calling it a god's birthday. Therefore, according to Joseph Campbell, by the fourth century, the Western Church had adopted December 25 as the date of the birth of Jesus Christ which under the Julian calendar was the day after the three days of (apparent) standing still of the sun, when the light begins to increase. Christ's birth now coincided exactly with the rebirth of the sun.

The symbols the ancients used at the Winter Solstice are very familiar to us. The main symbols of this bleak time of the year are a growing thing (tree or bush) and a burning thing (fire, sun, etc.). As Beverly Moon, in *An Encyclopedia of Archetypal Symbols*, tells us, these two images mesh to create a symbol, which expresses the idea of the spiritual as coming from above (heaven) and below (earth).

The most familiar symbol for this time of the year is, of course, the Christmas tree. According to Barbara Walker, in *The Woman's Encyclopedia of Myths and Secrets*, Prince Albert, the German bridegroom of Queen Victoria brought it to the English-speaking countries in the middle 19th century. Neumann tells us that, in Germany, the tree is a winter solstice symbol derived from the concept of the heavenly tree that shines by night. "It is also the soul tree of re-birth in which every creature that dies becomes a celestial light as a star in the eternity of the Great Round." It's a nice idea; no wonder it is so popular. Like all evergreens, such as the holly and ivy, the pine tree stood for a promise of eternal life because it kept its vital appearance even when other plants died off during the winter. Naturally this applied only to the living pine tree, lighted and decorated in the woods where it stood.

The menorah used at Chanukah, the Jewish holiday during this winter season, also contains the same elements as Christmas, the living tree that is holding burning candles. Chanukah, the Jewish Feast of Dedication, is called the Feasts of Lights. It is a holiday to celebrate a real historical event. The event was the rededication of the altar of the Temple at Jerusalem in 165 BCE (Before the Common Era) by Judah the Maccabee and his followers, after the altar was profaned by Antiochus IV. However, as Theodore Gaster in *Purim and Hanukkah* tells us, Chanukah was probably also more. The feast lasted eight days and repeated exactly the same dedication ceremonies as had taken place in the Temple's original dedication. For each successive day of the eight-day festival, an additional light is kindled. Since the holiday occurs on the 25th of Kislev, which is around the time of the winter solstice, it becomes easy to suspect the celebration had an earlier origin than the Maccabean victory. S. H. Hooke tells us, in *The Origins of Early Semitic Ritual*, that the custom of adding an additional candle each night may have been part of a solstice ritual to help the sun become stronger as it gains back its power.

The ancient Roman Saturnalia is another holiday with winter solstice beginnings. Saturn, the Roman name for the Greek Cronus, had a dual aspect. He was both awful as a God of Time and Death, and benign as a God of Agriculture—Ruler of the

Golden Age when all men lived in accord and were equal. His most popular festival contained both aspects. The holiday fell in December from the 17th to the 23rd. As befitting the dual aspects of the god, it was a topsy-turvy time, when the normal order of things was reversed. During this time, there were all kinds of fantastic amusements and great partying. Many feel that the carnival of Mardi Gras is a modern form.

The other side of the Roman Saturnalia came from Saturn being the Old Year ghost, the Lord of Death. The Lord of Death was the negative side of the summer sun. Rituals including human sacrifice were performed at the midwinter solstice so he would let spring return again. I felt the negative side of Saturn when I was at the Prado in Madrid, and first saw the Goya painting called "Saturn Devouring his Children." I was so overcome by the power and horror expressed in it, my knees shook and I had to sit for a few minutes to recover. Not too many paintings have that affect on me. Maybe that's why the revelry takes place, to cover over the horror of the passage of time.

Now I have an idea to propose: Since each of us on Planet Earth experiences the winter solstice, couldn't we develop a celebration to mark our common human experience of coming through winter? We could make it a community venture, play down or make private the individual religious events that divide and separate us. To do it, we would need many lights, sun-like objects like balls and oranges, jolly music, lots of babies and evergreens with which to celebrate life. Then we all could greet each other with a "Have a Happy Winter Solstice and a Healthy New Year!" and have it include all of us.

FOR FURTHER READING

Aveni, Anthony. *Empires of Time*. New York: Basic Books, HarperCollins, 1989. Print.

Baring, Anne, and Cashford, Jules, *The Myth of the Goddess*. London: Viking/Arkana, 1991. Print.

Bogdanovich, Peter. *A Year and a Day Engagement Calendar*. New York: The Overlook Press, 1994. Print.

Campbell, Joseph. *Mythic Image*. Princeton, NJ: Bollingen Series, Princeton University Press, 1974. Print.

Cooper, J. C. *The Aquarian Dictionary of Festivals*. Wellingborough, Northamptonshire, England: The Aquarian Press, 1990. Print.

Eliade, Mircea. *A History of Religious Ideas, Vol. I, From the Stone Age to the Eleusinian Mysteries*. Translated: W. Trask. Chicago: University of Chicago Press, 1978. Print.

Frazer, Sir James George. *The Golden Bough*. New York: Collier Books/Macmillan Publishing Co., 1922. Print.

Gaster, Theodore. *Herzl, Purim and Hanukkah*. New York: Henry Schuman, 1950. Print.

George, Demetra. *Mysteries of the Dark Moon*. San Francisco: HarperSanFrancisco, 1992. Print.

Graves, Robert. *Greek Myths, Vols. I and II*. New York: Penguin Books, 1955. Print.

Hooke, S. H. *The Origins of Early Semitic Ritual*. Oxford, England: Oxford University Press, 1938. Print.

James, E. O. *Prehistoric Religion*. New York: Frederick A. Praeger, 1957. Print.

Krupp, Dr. E. *Echoes of the Ancient Skies*. New York: Harper & Row, 1983. Print.

Moon, Beverly, Ed. *An Encyclopedia of Archetypal Symbols*. Boston: Shambhala Publications, Inc., 1991. Print.

Neumann, Erich. *The Great Mother*. Princeton, NJ: Bollingen Series, Princeton University Press, 1963. Print.

Sjoo, Monica, and Mor, Barbara. *The Great Cosmic Mother*. San Francisco: HarperSanFrancisco, 1987. Print.

Walker, Barbara. *The Woman's Dictionary of Symbols & Sacred Objects*. San Francisco: Harper & Row, 1987. Print.

———. *The Woman's Encyclopedia of Myths and Secrets*. San Francisco: HarperSanFrancisco, 1983. Print.

CHAPTER 15

The New Year Festival

NEW YEAR'S EVE IS A STRANGE EVENT; AND THE OLDER I get, I find the ways we mark this date even stranger and more artificial. So the question is "Why do we do this nonsense?" Bringing in the year 2000, with all of its extra festivities, only sharpened my feelings about the holiday. Yet when I started to examine what New Year festivities meant to people of the ancient world, I was fascinated to learn that celebrating the New Year has always taken place. What we do is what has always been done.

Religious historian Mircea Eliade, in his *Myth of the Eternal Return*, states that many of our modern festivals, though secular on the surface, still preserve a mythical structure and function. Examples he gives are the rejoicing over the New Year, or the festivities following the birth of a child. He feels these show the need to mark new beginnings. According to Eliade, there is no way to estimate how far modern man is aware of any mythological implications of his festivities; what matters is that such celebrations are still important to us in ways we do not understand.

For us moderns, New Year's Eve is only a party; there is no deeper meaning. The old year ends, the New Year begins, and that's it. We are completely unaware that the dining, dancing, drinking, general carousing and the obligatory countdown to midnight is a ritual humans have done at their New Year celebrations since the beginning of known civilization. It is a ritual the ancients felt made them part of the rhythms of time and of the world order.

According to Dr. E. Krupp, in *Echoes of the Ancient Skies*, the New Year in the ancient world was the time when unseen powers roamed the world and the dead returned to their old haunts. To banish these dark forces and restore order, the ancients marked the change from the old year to the new year by making loud noises, ringing bells, beating drums, cracking whips, rattling bamboo canes, letting off fireworks and sounding horns. It's not too much different from what we do today. When you live in Philadelphia as I do, New Year's Day is always a big and noisy event, because that is the day of the Mummers' parade. The parade, made up of all volunteers, starts early in the morning and frequently goes on until dark. It includes loud music, dancing to a special step called a Mummers' Strut, lavish costumes, cross dressing, lots of noise and much partying. It's a great parade and we Philadelphians love it. We have kept the customs alive, but we have lost their symbolic meaning.

In the ancient world, different cultures had New Year celebrations at different times of the year. When the celebration was held depended on what, for the community, was the most significant turning point in the year. It could be the beginning of the lengthening days during winter, the appearance of new plant life at the beginning of the growing season, or the rise of a particular star. For example, in ancient Egypt, the New Year began on July 20 when the Dog Star, Sirius, appeared in the sky as the seasonal sign that the Nile was going to flood.

The creation myths of different cultures clearly show the relationship of chaos and order. Chaos is the original state over which order must triumph. The chaos that precedes creation in

Genesis, and the Greek god Chaos from whom all other gods spring, are two familiar examples. According to Eliade, the orgy corresponds to the pre-Creation state of chaos. This is why New Year ceremonies include these rites of social confusion, sexual license and Saturnalia. In the New Year Festival, chaos reigns in the last days of the year, with carnival-type excesses of behavior, the reversal of all social order, the extinguishing of fires, and the return of the dead (represented by maskers). Ritual combats between two groups of actors are documented in Egypt, among the Hittites, and at Ugarit.

For most cultures, New Year's Day was a time of renewal and was always marked by a type of festival of rebirth. With these celebrations, the ancients felt they were helping to maintain the world's structure and stability. Doing proper acts at the proper time was what they did to help maintain the equilibrium of the whole cosmos. Since the ancients regarded each New Year as a completely new beginning, at the New Year the individual also made a fresh start, "turned over a new leaf," made resolutions. Many of us still do this; but I don't think we give much thought as to why.

For the ancients, the New Year meant much more than that. For them, according to Eliade in his book *The Sacred and the Profane*, it meant the past year and the past time was erased and a totally clean slate was created. To create that clean slate, rituals were created which expelled the old sins and demons and wiped out the past year and the past time. In ritual ceremonies, renewal is one of the key themes, particularly those ceremonies connected to the seasons of the year. Eliade lists the essential rites to mark the end of the old year and the beginning of the new as:

1. Purifications, confessing of sins, driving out demons, expulsion of evil;
2. Extinguishing and rekindling of all fires;

3. Masked processions (with the masks representing the souls of the dead);
4. Fights between two opposing teams;
5. An interlude of carnival, a reversal of the normal order, an orgy.

Through purifications, the ancients felt their individual sins and faults, as well as those of the community as a whole, were erased. In this way, all which time had soiled and worn was destroyed. Eliade also tells us that, by symbolically participating in the destruction and re-creation of the world, ancient humans felt they too were reborn, for now they began a new life. Rachel Levy, in *The Gate of Horn*, tells us that the New Year's Festival in Babylon dates back to the middle of the third millennium BCE. It included performances involving the defeat of the God, the death of his antagonist, his resurrection and marriage—all done for the country's prosperity. Hymns discovered on tablets in Syria suggest that similar dramatic performances were held there during the annual festivals. These rituals have been practiced as far back as we can trace written history. Sumer, where written history began five thousand years ago, is the earliest place we find the beginnings of many of our traditions. We have no clear idea why these particular traditions developed.

Ralph Abraham, in *Chaos, Gaia, Eros*, tells us that the Sumerians had three legends which the later Babylonians combined into their New Year festival, Akitu. These Sumerian legends are the sacred marriage, the defeat of chaos, and the eternal descent and return. The combination of the three in the Akitu became the defeat of the god, the death of his antagonist, and his resurrection and marriage. This was performed at the Babylonian New Year festival for the country's prosperity. Eliade tells us that, in the Akitu rituals, the sovereign played a considerable role, since he was regarded as the son of the divinity on earth. As such, he was responsible for the regularity of the rhythms of nature, and for the good estate of the entire society. Therefore, it is not surprising to find him playing an important role in the New Year ceremonies. The king began his reign on New Year's Day; and by virtue of his supernatural endowment at this birth and his sacred status with its ritual obligations, he was the most conspicuous figure in the annual festival.

During the Akitu, Babylonian priests recited the Creation story, the Enuma elis, several times. Then, as Diana Ferguson in *The Magickal Year: A Pagan Perspective on the Natural World* tells us, two groups of actors would mime the victorious birth struggles of the god Marduk from the formless, watery womb of Tiamat, the Mother Goddess, who was also known as the Deep. Another event that carried out the theme of the festival was a symbolic "sacred marriage" or *hieros gamos* of the king with a high priestess. This ritual reenacted the marriage of Dumuzi, a god associated with the growth of grain and dates, and Inanna, a goddess identified with fruitfulness and sex. According to Abraham, originally the festival was in the spring, to encourage the goddess to provide a good growth season. The sacred marriage passed from the Neolithic world and into historical mythology as the story of Babylonian Marduk and Ishtar, the Cretan Zeus and Hera, the Greek mysteries at Eleusis, and in the Psalms of the Old Testament. Some scholars feel that The Song of Songs from the Bible was written to accompany this type of ceremony. In Syria, tablets with hymns on them were discovered which suggest that, during their annual festivals, they had similar dramatic performances.

Part of the ancient rituals included ritual orgies to benefit the crops. According to Eliade, these imitated the sacred marriage of the king with the priestess. The ancients felt unlimited sexual frenzy stimulated the fertility of the fields. Because the orgy fit into the idea of chaos before the establishment of order, it reinforced the idea of the renewal of time and regeneration of the world that takes place at the New Year. It isn't clear why ancient man felt such rites were necessary for the earth to be fruitful. Somehow they overlooked the self-evident fact that, each spring, vegetation grows, whether humans did their rituals or not.

In Imperial China, the emperor was directly responsible for the ceremonial renewal of the world order. By his annual sacrifice to Heaven on the winter solstice, he was the link between cosmic harmony and the sun's yearly course. Heaven, in the official state religion, preserved the structure and stability of society by mandating the emperor's rule, and by creating order through cyclical celestial change. His performing the appropriate, and required, ceremonies helped the cosmos to continue. A belief in a participatory universe requires human beings to participate in specific, sacred roles to continue the world order. This explains why I found in a corner of the temple the old state weights and balances that are an essential part of ancient state order in the Forbidden City of Beijing, where the emperor performed his New Year rituals.

Gluttony, drunkenness, and other sins marked the turning of the year in ancient Rome. This was permitted on the theory that the next day brought the turning of a new leaf. The Roman New Year used to occur on the ides of March, during a season that later entered Christian tradition as the pre-Lent Carnival, Mardi Gras. Others cultures, however, celebrated the turning of the year around the winter solstice (the northern Yule).

Eliade, tells us that in ancient Israel, the New Year, the Feast of Tabernacles (Sukkot), took place on the fifteenth day of the seventh month (Deuteronomy 16:13) five days after the *iom ha-kippurim* (Leviticus 16:29) and its ceremony of the scapegoat. Before the adoption of the Babylonian calendar, the seventh month was the first month in the Jewish calendar, which made this the time of the New Year. Eliade tells us it was customary, at the time of the *ion ha-kippurim* for the girls to go outside the boundaries of the village or town to dance and amuse themselves, and it was on this occasion that marriages were arranged. (You can supply your own details.) But on this day, freedom was allowed for a number of excesses, a freedom we find all over the world in other New Year celebrations.

In northern Europe, the Celtic New Year took place in early November, on Samhain, which falls midway between the autumnal equinox and the winter solstice. The ancient world used a lunar calendar instead of the solar one we use. To them, the moon was more powerful than the sun. The lunar calendar counts a day as starting at nightfall, the eve, in this case October 31, Halloween. Celts called this day Samhain, a Festival of the Dead. To them, this was the time of the year when the veil between the living and the dead was at its weakest. In the minds of the ancient Celts, Samhain was a crucial and dangerous time. During the night, dangerous forces were abroad, supernatural beings and the dead roamed. Today, this tradition is celebrated as Halloween which is why even today, it is when ghosts and witches roam.

The lighting of the "new fire" is an important part of the Celtic New Year rites, as it demonstrates a new birth, a "new man." Eliade tells us the ritual extinguishing of fires is another way to end the existing forms (worn away by use) in order to make room for the birth of a new form, a new Creation. With the approach of Samhain, all the household fires and most of the ritual hearths of Ireland were extinguished to mimic the dying sun and the chaotic darkness to follow. Druid priests then rekindled the fire on the night before the Samhain sunrise, and sanctified it by burning sacrificial victims in the new bonfire. The Feast of Tara was also held at this time. This great general assembly and major festival was a time for enactment of new laws and for the settlement of accounts, debts, and litigation. Here the outstanding business of the old year was wrapped up and bundled away. Genealogies, records, and histories were brought up to date. Renewal, and therefore the world's renewal, was created by their ceremony of the "new fire."

In Scotland, where New Year has always been a more important festival than Christmas, a popular New Year custom is that of the First Footer. At midnight on New Year's Eve, the first-footer crosses the threshold, often bringing with him a sprig of mistletoe, or some gift of bread, salt, coal or kindling, and wishing all a happy New Year. Afterward there is much food and drink. Another simple, but highly symbolic, ritual is to open the back door at the stroke of midnight to let the Ghost of the Old Year out, and open the front door to allow the Spirit of the New Year in.

In China, the New Year festival takes place in early February at the first full moon. It is a time of merry-making, feasting and visiting friends. Houses are spring-cleaned, accounts are settled, business suspended, the paper gods of the door are renewed. Strips of red paper are printed with the characters for long life, health, wealth and happiness, together with spells to ward off evil spirits, and put on the doorposts and in the house. Red, the luckiest of colors, is predominant in all decorations in the house. Offerings are made to the gods and ancestors, new clothes are worn, drums and cymbals are sounded, and fireworks are let off in the streets. Fireworks and noise are essential to most Chinese festivals. Originally, they were to ward off evil powers. The festival ends with the Feast of Lanterns.

At Rome's New Year Feast of Atonement in March, people wore sackcloth and bathed in ashes to atone for their sins. Then as now, New Year was a carnival of eating, drinking, and sinning, on the theory that any sins committed would be forgiven 24 hours later by the atonement ritual. As the dying god of March, Mars took his worshippers' sins with him into death. Therefore the carnival fell on *dies martis*, the Day of Mars. In French the carnival day was Mardi Gras, "Fat Tuesday," the day of merrymaking before Ash Wednesday, which starts the 40 days of lent. The ashes symbolized atonement for sins; it was felt that bathing one's body in ashes would remove all traces of past transgressions.

Even today, we still have the need to start anew. The *Philadelphia Inquirer* in the winter of 2000 featured a lengthy article about how "cleansing" gets rid of negative energy. The ritual of "space-clearing," as spiritual practitioners call it, puts things in order. It is common in many cultures. In many cultures, "cleansing" means ridding the home of negative energy and spirits, not just dust and grime. One cleansed the home of negative energy and bad spirits by burning incense, opening windows, placing salt or rice in corners and cupboards, or setting glasses of water in each room. The practice, in its variety of forms, can be traced to dozens of cultures—from African and American Indian heritage to ancient Asian customs. In these cultures getting rid of clutter was necessary to prepare for the New Year in order to bring something new into their lives.

So, next New Year's Eve when you lift your glass, engage in some type of excessive behavior, get a fit of housecleaning, spend the day parading on the streets of Philadelphia in lavish costume, regalia and mask, or all of the above and more, remember you are part of a tradition that goes back to the beginning of civilization, and it's all O.K.

FOR FURTHER READING

Abraham, Ralph. *Chaos Gaia Eros.* San Francisco: HarperSanFrancisco, 1994. Print.

Aveni, Anthony F. *Empires of Time; Calendars, Clocks, Cultures.* Victoria House, Bloomsbury Square, London: I.B. Taurus and Co., Ltd. 1990. Print.

Cooper, J. C. *The Aquarian Dictionary of Festivals.* Wellingborough, Northamptonshire, England: The Aquarian Press, 1990. Print.

Eliade, Mircea. *A History of Religious Ideas, Vol. I, From the Stone Age to the Eleusinian Mysteries.* Translated: W. Trask. Chicago: University of Chicago Press, 1978. Print.

———. *The Sacred and the Profane: The Nature of Religion.* Translated from French: W. R. Trask. New York: Harvest/HBJ Publishers, 1957. Print.

———. *Cosmos and History: The Myth of the Eternal Return.* Translated: W. R. Trask. Princeton, NJ: Bollingen Series XLVI, Princeton University Press, 1954. Print.

Ferguson, Diana. *The Magickal Year: A Pagan Perspective on the Natural World.* London: B. T. Batsford Ltd., 1996. Print.

Hooke, S. H., Ed. *The Labyrinth: Further Studies in the Relation between Myth and Ritual in the Ancient World.* London: S.P.C.K., 1935. Print.

Krupp, E. *Echoes of the Ancient Skies.* New York: Harper and Row, 1983. Print.

Levy, Gertrude Rachel. *The Gate of Horn.* London: Faber & Faber, 1946. Print.

Neumann, Erich. *The Origins and History of Consciousness.* Princeton, NJ: Princeton University Press, 1970. Print.

Van Eenwyk, John R. *Archetypes & Strange Attractors.* Toronto, Canada: Inner City Books, 1997. Print.

Walker, Barbara. *The Woman's Dictionary of Symbols & Sacred Objects.* San Francisco: HarperSanFrancisco, 1988. Print.

CHAPTER 16

The Sacred Stones

STONES IN THE ANCIENT RELIGIOUS WORLD WERE A very serious business. According to Rachel Levy in *The Gate of Horn*, ever since the Stone Age, stones have been central in the observance of sacred rites. Even today, we respond to them. For example, a few years ago, the national press reported that officials at San Francisco's Golden Gate Park accidentally dumped one of their stone traffic barriers in an obscure part of the park. Stone traffic barriers are about four feet high and shaped like a large bullet. There, in the corner of the park, the barrier was found by local Hindus who treated it as a religious shrine and quietly left traditional offerings. After a while Buddhists, pagans and New Agers of many stripes also came. When one of the devotees was asked "Why?" the answer given was "God lives in the old traffic barrier." While to us that may seem to be an odd answer, in the ancient world this was an obvious fact, and one common to people in many lands.

It is no accident that stones are among the oldest symbols of the Great Mother Goddess. Erich Neumann, in *The Great Mother*, tells us that, in the days when the Great Mother Goddess was the deity, the ancients believed She lived in the stones. They were Her home. The stones were the bones of the earth; they were immortal and unchanging, a symbol of permanence.

The stones were the instruments of spiritual action, the centers of energy. Back in 1985, Don Robins, in *Circles of Silence*, wrote that, using ultrasonic detectors and Geiger counters, his team had discovered that certain of the ancient stone circles are electrically active and generate ultrasound when stimulated. Some feel that maybe, in ways we have lost, the ancients were able to feel this energy.

As the bones of the earth, the stones give off a profound vibration or resonance. The writers Monica Sjoo and Barbara Mor, in *The Great Cosmic Mother*, tell us all "primitive" people carry wishbones and healing-stones, talismans painted with magic symbols. Animals as well as humans seem drawn to tall stone pillars. Sick livestock rub against them in the countryside; and it is a timeless folk custom to touch the tall stones in order to become fertile, or to be cured of illness. The ancients regarded rock and stone as having the same significance as mountain and earth. Neumann tells us the ancients not only worshipped the mountain as the Great Mother, but they also worshipped the rocks. The stones of the Great Mother took many forms. There was the mountain, cave, stone pillar, and rock-seat, all as dwelling place, and incarnation of the Great Mother.

Many traditions and myths point to humankind's long-established habit of worshipping unusual stones as divine spirits, particularly the spirits of female ancestor or Goddesses. The writer Barbara Walker, in *The Woman's Dictionary of Symbols & Sacred Objects*, tells us the Hebrew *bethel*, house or embodiment of a deity, was a cognate of Greek *baitulos* or *baetyl*, a standing stone. Icelanders worshipped their Goddess Armathr, "Mother of Prosperity," in the form of a stone. "Holed stones" all over the world symbolized the womb and birth. In parts of Europe, women still pray to such stones, or crawl through them, as conception charms. Moabite Arabs used to call themselves *Beni Sahr*, Sons of the Rock. The prophet Jeremiah in Jeremiah 2:27 inveighed against his contemporaries' custom of calling stone one's mother "They said to wood, 'you are my father,' To stone, 'You gave birth to me,' While to Me they turned their backs." Certain myths even reveal that the people of the world were thought to have been born of stones in the beginning.

While the ancient peoples felt all stones had power, stones used for an altar could not be finely finished. Theodore Gaster, in *Myth, Legend and Custom in the Old Testament*, says that, all over the ancient world, rude stones were used in religious worship. He tells us that, in ancient times, all the Greeks worshipped unwrought stones instead of images. In the Stone Age, humans felt that they needed to make a home for their deity, such as a pillar of rough worked stone dedicated to worship. This is why Jacob, in Genesis 28:18, after his dream in which he saw God, set up his stone pillow as a permanent Beth-El, a House of God. Such sacred stones were places where with the right rituals people could summon the deity. A sacred stone had to be kept in its rough form and in direct contact with the earth. This might explain why, in Exodus 20:22, Moses was told, "And if you make for Me an altar of stones, do not build them hewn: for by wielding your tool upon it you have profaned it." Since making steps would require moving the stone from direct contact with the earth, this is most likely the basis for this tradition. The idea seemed to be that a dressed stone was the work of human hands, which made the stone less sacred. When worship took place on or before stones, the stone itself was not the object of worship; what was worshipped was the deity who lived in the stone. Levy tells us that communication with the deity in the stone was necessary. Sometimes the communication could be a touch, or a kiss; sometimes it was rubbing the stone with some medium such as oil or blood.

When meteorites fell from the sky, they became important in the ancient relationship between Heaven and Earth. Anne Baring and Jules Cashford, in *The Myth of the Goddess*, say the ancients considered the stones that fell from Heaven to be living, and still living after their fall. Of the meteorites that were worshipped, the best known are Cybele and the Black Stone of Mecca. Cybele, The Great Mother of the Phrygians of Western Turkey, was brought to Rome with great pomp in 204 BCE (Before the Common Era) during the last of the Punic Wars. Each year after that, the conical meteorite re-entered Rome in a procession in which she was carried in a chariot pulled by lions. Worship of her covered a large area of Europe. At one of the major crossroads in Madrid, Spain, I found the Plaza de Cibeles. In the center of the plaza stands a large marble statue of the Goddess Cybele standing in her carriage. I was told this is also the unofficial emblem of the city.

The Ka'aba in Mecca houses the meteorite called the Black Stone of Mecca. It is the focal point of the Muslim Hajj, or pilgrimage. According to Mircea Eliade, in *Patterns in Compar-*

Statue of the Goddess Cybele in her carriage

ative Religions, the Black Stone personified the Goddess and was sacred to the pre-Islamic Arabs; they dedicated it to the pre-Islamic Triple Goddess named Manat, Al-Lat (Allah) and Al-Uzza (the "Old Woman") worshipped by Muhammad's tribesmen. When Muhammad captured the shrine, he removed all evidence of earlier deities, then he dedicated the shrine to the one God of his monotheistic faith. What in antiquity had been a sacred feminine spot is now the holy center of patriarchal Islam. While its feminine symbolism has been lost, its priests, according to Esther Harding in *Woman's Mysteries, Ancient & Modern*, are still known as *Beni Shaybah*, which means Sons of the Old Woman.

Sacred stones took another form in the lands colonized by the Celtic tribes, that of the tradition of magical stones. Barbara Walker, in *The Crone*, tells us these Celtic tribes used sacred stones to announce acceptance of the ruler. They regarded the stones as the oracle of Mother Earth, and would not obey a candidate She refused. The best-known example of this is the "Sword in the Stone" story from the King Arthur tales. Remember, after everyone else had failed, Arthur, the boy, was easily able to pull the sword from the stone. This showed he was the rightful ruler of England. Another of the magic stones is the famous speaking stone of Blarney Castle. This is a block of bluestone built into the battlements of the castle. The stone has a long history recounting from what sacred place it might have come. Today, we say the stone gives the gift of "blarney" to those who kiss it.

The anointing stones used in Northern Europe are another form of sacred stones. These were sacred stones on which the candidates for kingship were required to stand, while the rituals to make them king took place. Anglo-Saxon kings stood on a stone at Kingston-on-Thames. Swedish monarchs also stood on a stone when they were installed at Uppsala. But the most famous of the anointing stones is the Scottish 400-pound red-gray sandstone Stone of Scone, which the English moved from Scotland when they subdued the Scots.

When there were Scottish kings, this was their coronation "seat." After their victory, the English mounted the throne of England on top of the stone, so for the past 750 years, when the monarch of England was crowned King in Westminster Abbey, he also, according to Scottish ancient tradition, was crowned King of Scotland. According to Walker, the Stone of Scone has a long history. Originally it was called the Hag of Scone. Scone is a town north of Edinburgh. The "Hag" part comes from the name the Saxons and Danes gave to their Grandmother-Goddess. Usually the Grandmother-Goddess, or Crone as most of the ancient communities called her, personified the powers of the Goddess that were concerned with wisdom, governance, death and rebirth among a lot of other things. Therefore, the stone recalls the ancient custom in which kings and chieftains were chosen by tribal councils of old women; they were inaugurated over sacred stones which then spoke aloud to show divine acceptance of each new ruler. Well, after keeping the Stone of Scone for 750 years, England finally decided to return it to Scotland, in 1996. This event was reported and followed in the international press. Some scoffers said the only reason England was returning it was to keep the Scottish Nationalistic Party from pushing to secede from England; but even so, most felt it was an important statement.

The Stone of Scone

According to Baring and Cashford, sometime during the fifth millennium BCE, and later, people with considerable engineering, geometric and astronomical skill raised giant stones to form circles, alignments and burial chambers—all of which required an extraordinary amount of time, labor and knowledge to build. Malta seems to have been an especially sacred island and has the remains of as many as thirty temples. The startling alignments at Carnac, in Brittany, have some 3,000 upright stones laid out in lines that extend for nearly 2½ miles (4 km) and may have formed part of a lunar observatory or a processional way for an unknown seasonal ritual. Ireland has some 500 megalithic tombs or temple-tombs, of which the great passage grave of Newgrange on the River Boyne is the most fascinating. Built over 5,000 years ago, about 3200 BCE, no Neolithic temple illustrates more graphically the response of the people of this time to the mysterious movements of the moon, stars and sun.

These old stone constructions, called megaliths, have always fascinated me. The word megalithic comes from the Greek words *mega*, meaning great, and *litos*, meaning stone. These things are big, in some cases one of the stones may weigh many tons. No one really knows their origins. These enormous stone monuments are older than the Egyptian pyramids or the first cities of ancient Sumeria. They are humanity's first architectural achievements. They are part of the reason I am so intrigued by the whole study of prehistoric subject matter. To me, they reveal a world I can't even imagine. First of all, these things are old beyond belief; and with each scholarly review they are dated even older. Second, we are taught civilization came to Western Europe very late and by way of the Middle East. Obviously the megaliths prove that isn't true, since they were built by people who not only understood advanced engineering and had considerable earth and stone moving skills, but also had knowledge of the stars, the moon, and the sun. They represent a particular era in the Great Goddess cult, which had the need to create symbolic images of their deity by combining large tracts of geographical area with architectural features.

The farming communities established in France and Spain during the sixth millennium BCE were earlier even than those established in Britain and Ireland. In France, there are over 5,000 megalithic tombs extending in a line from Brittany to the Mediterranean. The best-known French megaliths are probably the stones at Carnac in southern Brittany. I remember the awe I felt when I first saw the stones at Carnac. It was some years ago, and at that time no one, including my travel agent, had ever heard of Carnac. I was there because I read something about these weird things in the middle of Brittany. When I got there, they were even stranger than I imagined. Right in the middle of the farms of Brittany are more than 3,000 stones arranged in rows that stretch as far as the eye can see—nearly two and a half miles. The power of the place still holds. In those days, few people went to Carnac and since the area is so large, the stones were not roped off. You could go up to them and touch them. My husband climbed into one of the tombs and reported to me that, carved in the back wall, were marks we later learned were symbols of the Goddess. We were told that even today, girls with their bottoms bared slide down the stones, hoping the stones would make them pregnant. This part of southern Brittany, like the area around Stonehenge, was a major religious center, just as Jerusalem and the Vatican are now.

Ireland has some 500 megalithic tombs or temple-tombs, of which the great passage grave of Newgrange on the River Boyne is the most fascinating. My main reason for going to Ireland was to visit Newgrange, and it didn't disappoint. It is some 30 miles north of Dublin, in the center of a great concentration of Neolithic burial mounds. Stone Age farmers, who lived much as Irish farmers did until a century ago, built Newgrange over 5,000 years ago. Like the other sites, it is big. It is some 280 feet

Newgrange

in diameter, and stands on a low ridge about three-quarters of a mile north of the Boyne River. Faced in gleaming white quartz, it is visible for miles even on an overcast day.

Newgrange was both a house for the dead and a place of rebirth. It consists of an entrance with a long passage, which opened up into a chamber large enough to hold about twenty people. Going into it, I felt like I was entering a tomb; and then coming out through the long passage, I felt like I was being reborn. The bottom of the mound is marked by large stones called curbstones of which only some have survived. Possibly half of these curbstones are decorated with the triple spirals, lozenges and wave-like lines that today scholars consider to be signs of the energies of the Goddess. In front of the doorway lies a huge stone, decorated with these symbols. Local folklore said that when the sun rose at the winter solstice, it came through the roof box built over the entrance, went down the long passageway and lit the far end of the main chamber. All the scholars laughed at this idea; but on a winter solstice, one of them sneaked into the site to see what really happened. What happened was that the rising sun came in through the roof box and lit the far chamber exactly the way the folklore said it did. The rest of the year, this area is in darkness. What most fascinated me is that the passageway is built in such a way that, after some fifteen minutes or so of the rising sun, a curve in the passageway blocks the sun and the area is dark. Now to my mind, that is very fancy engineering for something built over 5,000 years ago.

After the Tower of London, Stonehenge, on the Wiltshire plain in southern England, is the sight visited by more sightseers than anything else in the British Isles. My eleven-year-old grandson endeared himself to me forever when he said he wanted to go to England to visit Stonehenge because he heard it was "mysterious." We are not sure of too much about Stonehenge, only that on the day of the summer solstice, the sun rises above the Avenue marked by the stones, and casts its shadow from the Heel Stone to the Altar Stone. We know also that, as the sun makes its annual passage across the sky, Stonehenge acts as a calendar, charting the passage of seasons. And that's about all we know. The rest is mystery and conjecture, with plenty of both. I remember when I first saw it. It just sits there, as it has for over 5,000 years, out in the middle of nowhere. I found myself filled with such wonder and awe, I ended up talk-

Stonehenge

ing to myself. Only the ruins of this great stone circle are left of a sacred circle built and altered over the course of several thousand years. It was started around 3000 BCE and rebuilt some twelve hundred years later. I always thought, as many of us do, that Stonehenge was built by the Celts and their Druid priests. Actually, it was built over a thousand of years before the Celtic period. We don't know exactly what rites took place at Stonehenge, but we do know the stones are arranged to make alignments with both the moon and the sun.

More perplexing to me than even Stonehenge is the huge Avebury complex some seventeen miles away. When I went there, not only did I know nothing about Avebury, I had never even heard of it. I didn't even know enough about it to see all of it. The complex is huge, the stone circle alone is so large it covers about 28 acres; and inside of it is a small village, at whose pub we had lunch. After lunch, we walked around the stones. What we missed was the ruined temple on the hill overlooking the river. We also missed the fifty-foot wide, mile and half long processional avenue that led from the temple to the Avebury stone circle itself. We did stop to see nearby Silbury Hill, the largest manmade hill in England, whose fascinating story I didn't discover until much later. We also missed the nearby 150-foot-long barrow or tomb. You can see we missed a lot. Generations were necessary to build a major complex like this. That this was a major religious center is very clear. It had to be very important to invest that much energy and time.

Today, what we can learn from all these stones is that the imagery the ancient humans first developed in the Stone Age survived, developed and lasted through all the various pre-historic cultures of Europe; even now, they remain objects of awe and reverence. Jungians say inside every human of today is a two million year old person. According to that theory, we still carry this ancient material in our myths, our art, much of our religion and most importantly, in our dreams.

FOR FURTHER READING

Baring, Anne, and Cashford, Jules. *The Myth of the Goddess.* New York: Penguin, 1991. Print.

Chevalier, Jean, and Gheerbrant, Alain. *A Dictionary of Symbols.* New York: Penguin, 1944. Print.

Dames, Michael. *The Avebury Cycle.* London: Thames and Hudson Ltd., 1977. Print.

———. *The Silbury Treasure: The Great Goddess Rediscovered.* London: Thames and Hudson, 1976. Print.

Eliade, Mircea. *Patterns in Comparative Religion.* Translated: R. Sheed. London: Sheed and Ward, 1958. Print.

Gaster, Theodore, H. *Myth, Legend and Custom in the Old Testament.* New York: Harper Torchbooks, 1975. Print.

Harding, M. Esther. *Woman's Mysteries, Ancient & Modern.* Boston: Shambala Publications, 1990. Print.

Levy, Gertrude Rachel. *The Gate of Horn.* London: Faber & Faber, 1946. Print.

Moon, Beverly, Ed. *An Encyclopedia of Archetypal Symbolism.* Boston: Shambala Publications, 1991. Print.

Neumann, Erich. *The Great Mother.* Princeton, NJ: Princeton University Press, 1963. Print.

Pollack, Rachel. *The Body of the Goddess.* Rockport, MA: Element Books, Inc., 1997. Print.

Robins, Don. *Circles of Silence.* Portland, OR: International Specialized Book Services, 1985. Print.

Sjoo, Monica, and Mor, Barbara. *The Great Cosmic Mother.* New York: Harper & Row, 1987. Print.

Scully, Vincent, Jr. *The Earth, the Temple and the Gods: Greek Sacred Architecture.* New Haven, CT: Yale University Press, 1964. Print.

Streep, Peg. *Sanctuaries of the Goddess, The Sacred Landscapes and Objects.* Boston: Bulfinch Press Books, 1994. Print.

Walker, Barbara. *The Woman's Dictionary of Symbols & Sacred Objects.* San Francisco: HarperSanFrancisco, 1988. Print.

———. *The Crone.* San Francisco: HarperSanFrancisco, 1985. Print.

CHAPTER 17

Sacred Dance

ONE OF THE STRANGEST STORIES IN THE BIBLE IS THE story of David dancing, with all his might, before God (II Samuel 6:14). David's wife, Michal, had trouble with it. too. She complained, not only of his dancing, but also of his "exposing himself in the sight of the slavegirls" (II Samuel 6:20). Why would David do this? All through the centuries, the rabbis have had trouble with this part of David's story. Yet, when we look closely at the most ancient functions of dance, we learn that it is one of the oldest forms of worship.

All over the world, the communities which existed before history was recorded usually worshipped the Great Goddess. Since they left no written language, all we know of these people comes through their traditions, legends and artifacts. In the past 100 years, we have added an enormous amount of newly-found original documents from the early historical period to our store of material. From this historical material, we are able to infer about some of the ancient behavior and belief systems.

Sacred dancing is very old. According to the Jungians, Baring and Cashford, dance, in all early cultures, was a way of communicating with the Goddess. Reaching Her through dance rituals brought Her into the midst of the moving forms. Erich Neumann, another Jungian, tells us it is particularly the orgiastic dances in which She was worshipped.

Scholars today tell us these ancient communities felt dance was magic, a way to communicate with the deity. Maria-Gabriele Wosien, the scholar and writer, felt that, through the magic created by the dance, the deity physically entered the body of the dancer, who then became at one with the divine. When the ancients participated in ritual dance worship, this was the transforming experience they were seeking. The magic of dance was created through a rhythmic release of energy, an ecstatic act, a release some scholars compare to the release found in the sex act. Such "sacred dancing" became the earliest form of prayer. Only much later does the spoken word replace dance as the major form of worship. Early people danced on every occasion. They made their sacred dances part of the rituals to obtain food, honor the dead, or assure good order in the cosmos. They also danced at events such as initiations, magic-religious ceremonies, and marriages.

Such dancing is not for an audience. While all present are involved, the dance itself is for the deity. It is always a community activity which unites sound, rhythm and movement. As such an activity, it is a very serious and intense affair. It was an important component of all religious rituals. Repetitive, rhythmical movement was thought essential to build up to the moment of ecstatic union with the deity, just as rhythmic sexual movements build up to orgasm. In many ways the two were interconnected. One purpose of ceremonial dance was the same as that of ceremonial sex: to imitate the process of cosmic creation, to renew the world by influencing divine powers to conceive, gestate, and bring forth yet again. I realized the intensity of this type of ritual when I watched a saint's feast day dance at a Hopi village in New Mexico. Large numbers of the tribe were involved in the dance, including a child not more than a toddler. Even though he was screaming his head off, and even though he was totally ignored by his dancing elders, I noticed he never missed a step. The dance, which monotonously went on and on, was to honor the village's female patron saint whose portrait stood in a central position.

Barbara Walker tells us the beat used in dance is the same beat felt by every fetus in the womb as s/he listens to the basic rhythm of his/her mother's heartbeat. Indian tantric tradition called this rhythm the "Nada," the "Sound of Power," or "Heartbeat of the Absolute." The idea of a heartbeat-dance at the core of all living things is clearly portrayed in the Indian "Dance of Shiva," which according to tradition took place in the "center of the universe" which also is the heart. The importance of dance is demonstrated by its role in many of the ancient creation stories. Walker also tells us that the early Goddess communities believed dance was a symbol of creation. They believed it was She who caused the initial creation of the universe by Her magic dance over the Water of Chaos, or Great Deep. It was said that Her rhythmic movements organized the as-yet-unformed element, making orderly patterns that the Greeks called diakosmos, the Goddess's ordering.

In addition, the deity was seen as the fertilizing power in nature, which creates life and brings the harvest. Wosein tells us the sprouting of the seed was seen as the fertilized womb. The dances, then, were acts of worship to help the crops grow. The fertilizing power in nature was worshipped as the manifestation of the god, bringing forth of fruit through the life-creating power of the Earth Mother. When the ancients leapt in the air around the young crops, they were forcing the seedlings to grow. The higher they jumped, the higher the plant could grow. Ancient people believed gestures were a form of imitative magic which brought power into the being of the worshipper. Dance gestures along with rhythm and music made the dance magic stronger.

The earliest dances were in the form of a circle. In the depths of a painted cave along the Spanish-French border, I saw footprints, some 20,000 years old, left by people doing some type of circular rhythmic movement. It is not surprising that circle dances were the first dances, as the circle always was a primary feminine sign. Early matrifocal villages had round hearths, round houses, and round fences. The circle itself was associated with the idea of a protected or consecrated space, a ceremonial space where all participants were equal. Pagan sacred dances were circular, and to this day, so are most European folk dances. Even today's wedding festivities seem to include some type of circle dance. In Cornwall, England, I saw several stone circles which local tradition called "dancing maidens." The story of these stone rings usually involved maidens, dancing at a holy time, who then were turned into stones. In the days of the Goddess, such rings, attended by priestesses, were powerful energy sources.

From ancient Crete, one of the last centers of Goddess worship, we have frescoes of sacred ring-dances being performed. Naked women dancers, arms linked, circled within a specified area. We don't know what these dances meant to the Cretans, but we do know dances from other areas had meanings we have either forgotten or ignored. Actually Marija Gimbutas, the archeologist, tells us the practice of the sacred ring dance can be as old as the Old Stone Age and surely continues throughout the New Stone Age, prehistory and history. Ring dances of naked women are found on ceramics of the second half of the 5th millennium BCE. Romanians call them "Hora vases" from the hora or "ring dance" still alive today. In Scottish dancing, Jill Purce tells us that every "turn" is a recreation of the Goddess's original cosmic dance of creation (clockwise) and dissolution (counterclockwise).

The sexiest dances of the ancient world must have been the May Day Dances. In the Celtic calendar, May Day is the first day of summer, a crucial time in the life of the crops. The ancient May Day Dances were full of raw energy and a lot of passion. These were needed to accomplish the goal of the dances, which

The Maypole dance

was to reenergize the earth so the crops would grow. Walker tells us, "It was a time of sexual license, symbolizing nature's fertilization; a honeymoon when marriage bonds were temporarily forgotten and sexual freedom prevailed in rural districts all the way up to the sixteenth century." It was the Maypole dance, which was the origin of the square dancer's Grand Right and Left, as men and women alternately passed in and out of each other's circles, winding the ribbons around the pole. The weaving of the long streamers created a continuous pattern without stops or breaks. This endless, "gateless" line was thought to form a barrier against evil influences. Today, even though the serious religious aspects of the festival have disappeared, the dance still keeps its original form. In England, children now hold the long streamers attached to the top of the pole. As they dance round the Maypole, the ribbons are twined round it, to be untwined when the dancers reverse. I watched a group of school children in the English countryside practicing weaving their ribbons from the Maypole; it was a charming picture, but a much watered down experience from the ancient May Day dances.

From other parts of the earth came different ways of dancing. In Greece and Rome, members of the cult of Dionysus or Bacchus would dance while celebrating their rites under the influence of sacred intoxicants such as wine, ivy or mushrooms. According to Sjoo and Mor, one of these is the ecstatic dancing of the bacchantes, wild women intoxicated by chewing ivy leaves and also the mushroom, sacred to Dionysus. "The Bacchantes or Thracian Maenads (mad women) were the daughters of the Great Mother—her 'white wild maids,' possessing the magical power to make the whole earth blossom." If we are to believe the various legends and stories of these celebrations, things frequently got very wild. These celebrants believed it was through their uninhibited behavior that they could experience in full, the creative power of the god.

Other forms of ecstatic dancing come to us from the Near East, Thrace, and the Mediterranean. Their stories are in Greek legend and history. The story of the Great Goddess Cybele comes from this area. She was one of the many forms of the Great Mother. Her cult started in Asia Minor, then spread to Greece and Italy in the Roman era. As Wosein tells us, as part of the celebrations in Her honor, Her priests would dance into a wild ecstatic trance. The wild noise of drums, cymbals, pipes and rattles accompanied the dancer's frenzied movements, cries and shouts. At the climax of this ritual dance the priests often castrated themselves. By this act they identified with their Goddess, their castration was the sign of total surrender to Her.

Sufi dervishes today claim their hand clapping, dancing, whirling, and singing are involuntary expressions of the divine power showing itself through their bodies. Sjoo and Mor, in *The Cosmic Mother*, tell us this way of life comes from the earliest days. Through their dancing, the Sufis reach self-realization and joyfully experience union with the larger Self of the universe. Sufi dervishes in their dance rites go into swoons. They sing, sigh, weep, cry, sway from side to side, thrust knives into their flesh, and burn themselves in the heat of delirious passion.

In the winter of 1996, I was in Aruba during Carnival, where I watched part of the local parade. This was different from anything I had ever seen. The music had an overwhelming beat, the same pounding beat for the entire parade. The beat matched my heartbeat. I actually could hear and feel my beating heart. The effect made me feel as if I were pulsating as one with the crowd, a somewhat unsettling and scary sensation. The marchers, lavishly costumed, were more bare than dressed, and the movements, to say the least, were stimulating. There was ongoing action between the bystanders and paraders, and the alcohol flowed. The effect was loud, raucous, and very sexy. And we were only there as the parade was getting started. I doubt that many participants at this event slept alone that night. For those of us who live in the sober modern world, maybe our spiritual lives would deepen with a few wild orgies.

Another form of dance was based on the spiral symbol. Both single and double spirals were among the most sacred signs of Neolithic Europe. They appeared on megalithic monuments and temples all over the continent and the British Isles. The spiral was connected with the idea of death and rebirth. When following a spiral, the ancients felt they entered the mysterious earth womb, went to its core, and passed out again by the same route. Robert Graves tells us that many of the European folk dances derived from pagan days imitated this movement, using a spiral line of dancers circling into a center and out. This was the traditional formula for walking a labyrinth or maze. In British country villages such maze-type dances, called "Troy Town," were danced at Easter.

Plutarch describes an early Greek maze dance in his *Life of Theseus*. According to him, Theseus, after slaying the Minotaur in the Labyrinth of Knossos, left Crete and sailed his ship into the harbor at Delos. There he offered a sacrifice to the god Apollo, and with his companions, performed a dance that imitated the circular pathways of the labyrinth, into the center and back again, the direction of involution and death followed by evolution and birth.

Dance played an important role at funerals. While this may seem odd to us, to the early communities according to Wosein, it was based on the belief that since death is only another aspect of life, it is the duty of the living to help the dead to their resurrection. The dances of death then, which are frequently labyrinthine or circular in character, are essentially dances of rebirth. Funeral dancing was given emphasis by strong rhythms, loud musical accompaniment and the wailing of the mourner. One of the ancient dances associated with funeral ceremonies were the "limping dances" described by Graves.

An example of one is described in I Samuel 15:32. Here Agag, the King of the Amalekites, who was defeated by Saul, is led into the presence of the prophet Samuel. He comes walking "delicately" and exclaiming, "Bitter indeed is death." According to Theodore Gaster in *Myth, Legend and Custom in the Old Testament*, "delicately" really means "with limping gait." Gaster tells us the reference is to a Semitic funeral custom where the mourners shuffle around the casket with a peculiar limping or hopping step. Ancient Hebrew dirges, possibly because they had to accompany this limping dance, had a different meter than other Hebrew verses. This "limping meter," which is characteristic of Hebrew dirges, is found in the first three chapters of the Book of Lamentations.

From all of this it becomes clear that, traditionally, dance is not only movement, but also a means to create energy and a power that ancient civilizations recognized and honored as religious and spiritual. Interestingly today, the most current scientific theories support the concept that the basic power of the world is the energy of movement. Developing this idea creates a situation in which both physicists and mystics alike view reality in terms of flow and movement, change and transformation.

It appears the ancients knew and understood what modern scientists just now are discovering. As King David must have known, it is all in the dance.

FOR FURTHER READING

Baring, Anne, and Cashford, Jules. *The Myth of the Goddess*. New York: Penguin, 1991. Print.

Cirlot, J. E. *A Dictionary of Symbols*. New York: Philosophical Library, Inc., 1962. Print.

Dames, Michael. *The Avebury Cycle*. London: Thames and Hudson Ltd., 1977. Print.

Eliade, Mircea, *The Myth of Eternal Return, or Cosmos and History*. Princeton, NJ: Bollingen Series XLVI, Princeton University Press, 1965. Print.

Frazer, Sir James George. *The Golden Bough*. New York: Macmillan Publishing Co., 1922. Print.

Gaster, Theodore H. *Myth, Legend and Custom in the Old Testament*. New York: Harper Torchbooks, 1975. Print.

Graves, Robert. *The White Goddess*. New York: HarperCollins, 1966. Print.

James, E. O. *The Cult of the Mother-Goddess*. New York: Barnes & Noble, 1994. Print.

Jeanes, Rosemary. "Labyrinths," *Parabola*, Volume IV, No. 2, May, 1979. Print.

Neumann, Erich. *The Great Mother*. Princeton, NJ: Princeton University Press, 1963. Print.

Pagels, Elaine. *The Gnostic Gospels*. New York: Vintage Books, 1979. Print.

Purce, Jill. *The Mystic Spiral, Journey of the Soul*. London: Thames and Hudson, 1974. Print.

Sjoo, Monica, and Mor, Barbara. *The Great Cosmic Mother*. New York: Harper & Row, 1987. Print.

Walker, Barbara. *The Woman's Dictionary of Symbols & Sacred Objects*. San Francisco: HarperSanFrancisco, 1988. Print.

West, John Anthony. "Reflection on Reflection." *Parabola*, Vol. IV, No. 2, May 1979. Print.

Wosein, Mariea-Gabriele. *Sacred Dance, Encounter with the Gods*. London: Thames and Hudson, 1992. Print.

CHAPTER 18

The Energies of the Earth

MOST OF US RAISED IN OUR MODERN WESTERN TRADItion of rational thinking, which emphasizes logic, proof, and science, do not believe the Earth is alive and has energy of its own. People of the ancient world thought differently. They believed not only was the Earth alive, but also that it gave off energies which the people of that time could and did use. While this idea may seem foolish to us, there is a large body of folktales and hard-to-explain practices and events to support it. For example, my mother-in-law felt she had ESP (extrasensory perception); she felt she always knew when one of her family, no matter how far away had hit trouble. While the family didn't believe she had ESP, she really was good. It came from somewhere!!

The trouble is, none of this can be verified. As Frances Hitching, who wrote *The Mysterious World, An Atlas of the Unexplained*, says, there are no written records of what went on in megalithic time, and the stories are not specific enough to be sure. But something else does seem to operate in the world, something outside the current body of science that would explain a pet dog finding its master over the distance of a continent, or a psychic describing what is happening hundreds of miles away, some unknown energy must be allowing this to happen.

With this theory of earth energy goes the notion that many of the old sacred sites in Europe and Asia, the ancient monuments, circles, and megaliths (standing stones), were built to channel the earth energy for the useful good of the community. Unfortunately there are no written records from those early days, nothing that Western logic can accept as proof, so take a deep breath as we suspend disbelief and step into the ancient world.

Scholars believe that early humans felt tied and dependent on Mother Earth, who was the universal deity; and as such, each part of Her was sacred. The folklore, legends and traditions indicate they particularly felt Her spirit around sites untouched by human activity. Examples of such would be springs, trees, hills, unworked stones, rocks, caves and rivers. They chose these active energy sites for special reverence and these were the places where the ancients built their sacred buildings. In almost every area where standing stones and circles are found, variations of the same legends are told which connect the megaliths with giants, fairies, treasure as well as power, healing or sanctity.

Nigel Pennick, author of *Earth Harmony: Places of Power, Holiness & Healing*, tells us the old nature religions, which developed when the world was solely agricultural, developed a set of practices and rituals. The practices of the nature religions required rituals at sites where the spirit of Mother Earth was manifested. Honored by continuous traditional use, these sites have remained sanctified up to the present day, though sometimes in unlikely guises. Today, we regard this honoring as superstition. We find it difficult to believe illiterate and supposedly primitive farming communities were able to lay out their various monuments and temples in vast coordinated schemes. We are puzzled by monuments such as Stonehenge. Is it just a monument, or is it also a focal point in a huge network of interconnected sacred sites, whose purpose today has been forgotten?

Planning such as this is part of an old science called geomancy. It concerns itself with the correct siting, proportion and orientation of buildings and landscape as important and necessary to maintain the earth's harmony. Geomancy, once universally known, was still widely practiced in Europe until the late eighteenth century. Today it is still used in Taiwan and Hong Kong. In almost all countries of the world geomancy remains can still be found in the landscape, architecture, ritual and folklore.

When the religion practiced at a sacred site is replaced by another form of worship, the site still is sacred, but now tells a different story. So by following the stories you can follow the history of the sacred sites. Jean Shinoda Bolen, in her book *Crossing to Avalon*, tells us that in England, for example, sacred sites that once were sacred to the Goddess usually became churches built and named for Saint Michael, or chapels built in honor of Mary. Mary is an easy one to figure, but Saint Michael needs a bit of explaining. He usually is described as stamping on a serpent, a symbol of the Goddess, and also a symbol for the energy current or ley lines (as they are called in England) that "snake" under the ground at sacred sites. In China, such lines are known as lung-mei, the paths of the dragon. To this day before buildings are constructed in modern Hong Kong, Chinese geomancers are consulted about these dragon currents.

Areas where the energy is strongest became, in our word usage, power points. All over the world, whether in Western Europe or China, the images associated with this energy are similar. Bolen tells us that in a culture which respected the Earth, the dragon was considered benevolent. But in the Judeo-Christian cultures, where the Earth (and goddesses and women) needed to be tamed and subjugated, dragons, snakes, and serpents were feared—stamped out by Saint Michael, driven out by Saint Patrick, or killed by Saint George. Today, many of these sites are connected to myths of magical power or force, a force which dowsers and others who explore these energy sources claim they are able to sense.

Dowsing, often called "water divining," is a way of divining sites of energy by means of the rod. It is an ancient skill for finding water and other things. Dowsers use metal rods, (wire hangers work fine), forked hazel twigs or pendulums. When the object being sought is nearby these instruments will respond—jerk, rotate or swing—in the hands of the dowser. It is an art which goes back into the distant past, and while it seems to work, no one has a clue as to how. As a result, most of us just laugh at the whole idea. Those who don't laugh offer the explanation that there is some unknown wave or emanation, so far undetectable by scientific methods, but which certain sensitive people are able to pick up. According to Hitching, in this theory, every single object in the world—now and in the past—emits its own wave pattern. This wave pattern is what dowsers, acting like superb radio receivers, are able to tune in to. Even though most of us find the idea very strange, dowsers feel dowsing is an absolutely natural ability which people always had, but which, over time, was lost through inactivity or suppression. Most people, they say, with practice, can usually master the skill. Dowsers themselves do not know where their skill comes from. An uncluttered and open mind is all they say is needed. Many believe that ancient humans had a natural ability to dowse, and used it as a matter of course in everyday life, for what purpose nobody really knows. The phenomenon cannot be properly explained.

The first time I actually saw someone using a dowsing rod was some years ago in England. During a hiking trip, our English leader was showing off to the group of Americans his abilities to use a dowsing rod. To our group of unbelievers, it was really odd; but England, a country with a much older civilization than ours, is far more accepting of diverse and offbeat ideas than we are. Using an old wire hanger, the dowser hit something because the rod responded with some movement in his hands. Different dowsers use different grips, and some are specialized in searching for particular things. Water dowsing is the most common, but underground electric power cables, mineral ores, lost objects, even lost people, are all on record as having been found by dowsing. What the best dowsers can achieve is certainly beyond scientific explanation. To be able to do this certainly feels like magic, so perhaps it is not surprising that in the United States dowsing is widely known as water-witching.

As Hitching tells us, the gifts shared by dowsers and other sensitive people are not intellectual or rational. They come from some sensitivity within the person. This isn't really that odd, since most creatures, from animals to insects, seem to have some instinct about unseen currents—such as the ones used in migration or homing instincts. Would man alone have developed without the ability common to other animals to "know" and "feel" things without thinking about them? Hitching tells us that many feel that megalithic man had a natural ability to dowse. Exactly what ancient man used it for is sheer speculation.

To make matters even more interesting, researchers recently have determined that a large number of the ancient megalithic standing stones circles of Europe are located on the intersection of two or more of these underground dowsing lines. According to the theories of recent thinkers, the energy currents created by the intersections would have been known by the dowsers, diviners and priests of the ancient age who built these stone circles. Thus, to the ancients, the sites would represent important sources of earth energy, and the circles would be built to mark the sites.

Even more odd are the recent findings of scientists, described by Don Robins in his book *Circles of Silence*, who, while working with some of these stone circles, found that at certain times of the day (early morning) and of the year (March and September) they were able to measure some sonic activity, unusually high radioactive output and even an ultrasound barrier, which is a cone of silence inside the stone circles. Outside of the circle, there was sound. Now the question is, was this accidental or did ancient humans know about the energies inside the stone circles and plan for and use them in some way?

Many of the same researchers who discovered and investigated the megalithic monuments in England felt these monuments were also, in some mysterious way, connected across the country to each other. According to this theory, the ancient sites were deliberately placed in the landscape to form a network of straight alignments which might stretch for many miles. We know that many of the megalithic sites do fall into straight lines. It is as though there was an invisible pattern of connecting straight lines built into the landscape which determined where the ancient monuments should be placed. In England these connecting lines are called ley lines.

It was many years ago I first heard about ley lines. For whatever reason they have fascinated me all these years, even though I still haven't made up my mind as to whether I believe in them or not. They were "big" in the late 1960s when they became part of the popular culture. They are mentioned in the lyrics of rock songs and the underground newspapers of the '60s and '70s. They also became part of the general questioning of the established attitudes and standards of that time. So exactly what is a ley line?

According to Nicholas Mann in *The Isle of Avalon*, one school of thought says a ley line is a straight alignment across the landscape between human-made sites, such as a standing stone, a mound, a temple, or a road. The line can also contain natural sites, such as a hill, a spring, or a notch on the horizon. Another school of thought says a ley line is an "energy line" that need not necessarily be straight. Nor do the sites on the line have to be contemporary with each other. In this case one can have a church, an Iron Age camp, and a Neolithic standing stone as part of the alignment. According to the theory, the ley line creates a "ley corridor" along which some kind of earth energy travels, like light along a fiber-optic tube. This school of thought believes that, at some time or another, people knew all about these kinds of energy and could apply it for various purposes. From the stories and legends, it would seem that the energy was used to maintain harmony and fertility within the ancient communities. Today, the academic establishment sees the whole concept as totally off the wall. Nonetheless, leys are studied by mathematicians, engineers, architects, geographers, and a few historians; they also attract dowsers, flying saucer investigators, mystics, astrologers and psychics. One man's proof of a ley line is another man's doubt.

About ten years ago on a trip to England, as our group was leaving Stonehenge, I asked our quite knowledgeable guide what he knew about ley lines. With vehemence not exactly appropriate for dealing with a client, he informed me he would have nothing to do with that rubbish. I responded that I didn't ask him what he thought of it, I only asked what he knew. When he just sneered at me, I decided he wasn't going to give any information. The whole subject of ley lines does bring out strong emotions from the many who don't believe; yet there is a large body of those who do believe. For example, on a 2007 trip to Stonehenge with a young grandson, our guide brought along several pieces of wire hangers. Then, at a juncture of two of the stones, he demonstrated to us how the wires jumped in his hands. We each had a turn doing this and in each case there was a strong reaction. Maybe even the guides are beginning to become more receptive to "strange ideas."

According to the believers of ley lines, the site for an ancient sacred place such as Stonehenge wasn't picked by chance. When the leaders of the ancient religions made their choices they took into account their understanding of the earth, the stars and the stones which stood between the two. It is as though the thousands of stone circles scattered across Europe were placed there in combination with the water sub-courses and the ley lines of energy that criss-crossed the land.

Until recently, the idea that prehistoric man could have laid out—or even wanted to lay out—such precise alignments on the landscape was regarded as impossible. Those early occupants of human history were seen as ignorant, ape-like, at best, and certainly mathematically backward. However, in recent years we have learned a lot more about the ancient people of many thousand years ago. One of the major things we have learned is the ancients knew far more about mathematics and astronomy than we could ever had imagined. We have also learned there was much more communication and trade between the early communities than we had previously thought.

The whole ley controversy-what are they for, where did they originate, what do they mean—continues without clear answers. But what we can be sure of is that they were "visible" to the ancients as a part of the holy connection between humans and nature, humans and their planet. As Sara Ann Osmen, author of *Sacred Places, A Journey into the Holiest Lands*, tells us, the Mother Earth Goddess, with her meridians of power and force, was as much alive as any human that occupied Her land.

The story of the ley, or dragon, currents does not end in Europe. The Australian Aboriginals have in their culture an idea of energy lines similar to ley lines. Mann tells us they believe the landscape was crossed in the time of creation, in dreamtime, by the creative spirit ancestors. As each ancestor, human and animal, moved over the landscape, they sang it into existence. The Aborigines call the paths of the ancestors songlines. By walking the lines, by "singing up the landscape," by visiting each site, by painting it, or by drawing it in the sand, the energies of that place and of the particular quality connected with it can be increased. The Far East can also boast all manner of similar phenomena. In the Valley of the Thirteen Tombs near Beijing, burials are not permitted on the path called a "processional way" for fear of damaging the energy lines of the earth currents beneath.

In Hong Kong and Taiwan, people's lives are affected, even today, by the principles of what has been called the earth spirit, a natural energy that makes people decide where is the right place to site their sacred buildings. To these Chinese, this art is known as Feng Shui (pronounced fung shway), which today is becoming popular in the West.

Nigel tells us that in this world view, doing things such as not siting a building correctly was not only a failure for the building, but would bring unfortunate results in the future. On the other hand, if the correct manner was applied at the right place and time, the procedures would reflect not only what had gone before, but also what was about to happen. This is the philosophy that underlies the Tarot, the I Ching and other forms of divination which involve the creation of patterns to foretell the future. The beans, stones, yarrow stalks or cards used for divination assume pattern, according to the influences in the universe at that moment. In the same way, the positioning of houses or temples had to be done to reflect the state of the universe at the time they were founded. Then, they were in harmony with the cosmic order, and not disruptive of the finely tuned balance of the cosmic energy.

A. T. Mann tells us, in *Sacred Architecture*, that Feng Shui is not a religious belief but a technique which allows people to use earth energies to benefit their lives. Followers believe it has a proven ability to bring good luck and prosperity in the areas of health, wealth, career, and relationships. It does this by creating balance with Nature in our living spaces to ease stress and create more joy. Before you dismiss it as totally silly, remember it is taken very seriously in Asia. In Hong Kong, the beautiful China Bank building, designed by I. M. Pei used the theories of Feng Shui. Basic to Feng Shui is the belief that the earth is a living entity animated by spirit. This spirit flows in channels through and on the surface of the earth. Through the energy it is possible for men to experience the presence and local character of the earth spirit, to work to bring our human ways into harmony with it, and even to influence its flow.

Mann says a system called Lung-mei, which mean Dragon Paths, was used by the Chinese empire to help concentrate power in the imperial capital by diverting the natural, serpentine streams of earth energy into long straight channels and directing them towards the emperor at the seat of government in Beijing. These straight channels then were kept clear of buildings or tombs so the energy flow remained clear. Some stretches were paved and became used as roads; others ran invisibly across the country. The course of the channels was marked by obelisks, ceremonial bridges and temples built so their main axes coincided with the alignment. In this way the spiritual energies of the earth, generated in mountain temples and monasteries, sustained the emperor. In the empires of antiquity Feng Shui was a state-controlled science, directed by the emperor himself, whose main responsibility was to observe meticulously the rituals connected with it.

Straight lines on the landscape have been a feature of many ancient civilizations, and their remains can be seen in many places. In many countries, there may be a network of mystical routes, sometimes used only at festivals or ceremonies, or for ritual journeys as funeral routes. A memory of them is contained in the legends found all over of underground tunnels linking ancient sites. Even today their reputation remains as spirit paths or as haunts of fairies and ghosts, places to be avoided on particular days of the year. Since the earliest times, straight tracks and roads were associated with the idea that leadership is the ability to set people or things in a straight line. For example, in English "ruler" means both a straight-edged measuring rod and a person with the power to command.

In this way, the ancient religions used their belief in power and energy of their Great Goddess, Earth. They knew the water courses and leys even if we, with our modern eye, cannot see them. Our need for rational explanation perhaps leads us up the wrong path. Leys may be connected to, or associated with, irrational explanation. Irrationality is nothing more, after all, than the presently unexplained. What is irrational to us was clearly wholly understandable to our ancient ancestors. To our ancient ancestors, the earth was alive with energies which beat across its surface.

FOR FURTHER READING

Bolen, Jean Shinoda. *Crossing to Avalon.* San Francisco: HarperSanFrancisco, 1994. Print.
Crisp, Roger. *Ley Lines of Wessex.* Wiltshire, England: Wessex Books, 1998. Print.
Hitching, Francis. *The Mysterious World, An Atlas of the Unexplained.* New York: Holt, Rinehart and Winston, 1979. Print.
———. *Earth Magic.* New York: William Morrow and Co., 1977. Print.
Mann, A. T. *Sacred Architecture.* New York: Barnes and Noble, 1993. Print.
Mann, Nicholas R. *The Isle of Avalon: Sacred Mysteries of Arthur and Glastonbury Tor.* St. Paul, MN: Llewellyn Publications, 1996. Print.
Michell, John. *The Earth Spirit: Its Ways, Shrines and Mysteries.* London: Thames and Hudson, 1975. Print.
Osmen, Sarah Ann. *Sacred Places, A Journey into the Holiest Lands.* New York: St. Martin's Press, 1990. Print.
Pennick, Nigel, *The Ancient Science of Geomancy: Living in Harmony with the Earth.* London: Thames and Hudson Ltd., 1977. Print.
———. *Earth Harmony: Places of Power, Holiness & Healing.* Milverton, Somerset, England: Capall Bann Publishing, 1991. Print.

———. *Leylines*. London: Wedenfeld & Nicolson, The Orion Publishing Group, 1997. Print.

Williamson, Tom, and Bellamy, Liz. *Ley Lines in Question*. Kingswood, Surrey, England: World's Work, 1983. Print.

CHAPTER 19

Tragedy

COMING DOWN A MOUNTAIN IN CRETE, WHILE I WAS half asleep in the bus, the tour guide suddenly pointed to two fairly large circles on each side of the road. These, she said, were threshing floors, where in the very early days of Greece, priests, dressed in goatskins as part of a ritual ceremony, came to sing praises to their god, Dionysus. She then told us that the name of the hymn they sang, *Tragos* (which means "goat song") is the source for the word tragedy. What!! How did all these things mesh together; threshing floors, Dionysus, goats, songs and tragedy? But they did. You must admit though, it is an odd combination.

Let's first look at threshing floors. They are a very utilitarian place where ancient people separated the grain from the chaff at harvest time. A most important place, essential in the ancient community, they are found all over the world. For a long time now they have fascinated me as I keep finding them in the strangest places. Threshing floors show up frequently in all kinds of ritual and religious events. In the Old Testament, there is the threshing floor of Atad, where Joseph mourned Jacob (Genesis 50:11); the threshing floor where Uzzah touched the ark and died (II Samuel 6:6); and the mention also in I Samuel 23:1 when David is told the Philistines are plundering the threshing floors. Then, there is the story of Ruth going to Boaz as he slept on the threshing floor (Ruth 3:2–9). But to me, the most interesting Bible reference is II Samuel 24 and I Chronicles 13. This is the story of how David, to stop a pestilence brought by the Lord, bought the threshing floor of Araunah the Jebusite to use as an altar for sacrifices. Later, II Chronicles 3:1 tells us that this is the spot where Solomon built the Temple on Mount Moriah. So the question, is why does the useful area the ancients used for preparing grain appear in so many religious situations?

The religious rituals of ancient Greeks also used threshing floors. Jane Harrison, in *Prolegomena to the Study of Greek Religion*, tells us they even had a threshing festival called *Haloa*, which means threshing floor. The Haloa, a women's festival, which went back to the ancient days of the Great Mother, honored Demeter, the Greek earth mother goddess and goddess of grain. Originally during the festival, circular harvest dances were performed and sporting events took place. To this day, the great round threshing-floor found in most Greek villages, like the one the tour guide showed, is the scene of the harvest festival. Carl Kerenyi, in his book *Dionysos, Archetypal Image of Indestructible Life*, tells us the round stage of the Greek theater came from these circular threshing floors.

Strangely enough, the Greeks celebrated the Haloa on the 26 of the month of Posedeon (December–January), too late in the winter to be threshing grain. Normally, in ancient days, threshing followed as soon as possible after cutting the grain. After the grain was threshed, it was separated from the chaff by blowing it in the air on the open threshing-floor. Mid-winter is no time, even in Greece, for an open-air operation. How this came to be, according to Harrison was simple; the shift of date from fall to winter was due to the power of the worship at the arrival of the god Dionysos.

The cult of Dionysus came to Greece before the end of the second millennium BCE. Joscelyn Godwin, in *Mystery Religions in the Ancient World*, tells us his cult came from Thrace. According to Walter Otto, in *Dionysus, Myth & Cult*, he was the god of ecstasy and terror, of wildness and of the most blessed deliverance—the mad god whose appearance sends mankind into madness. Godwin says, ". . . his worship spells orgies and drunkenness; he personifies the irrational and uncontrollable urges of man and beast." He was the child of Zeus and Semele, a mortal woman, who was killed. Then Zeus inserted the fetus into his thigh until he was ready to be born, a second time.

His festivals were in mid-winter when the wine vines were cut and the wine tasted. His was such a powerful presence that his festival took over the threshing floor festival of Haloa. The festival of the corn goddess blended with worship of Dionysos at the time of the cutting of vines. This is how the strange idea of a winter threshing festival developed. Actually it wasn't too strange for the festivals to merge, as the basic concept for both cults was the idea of the New Birth. According to Godwin, Dionysus was the god of the cycles of the earth. One year his death was commemorated, the next year his resurrection, in a two-year cycle of Dionysian festivals.

Today we know Dionysus as the Greek god of wine. He was much more to the Greeks. For the Greeks, Dionysus was the god of ecstasy and terror, and of wildness and madness. According to Leonard Shlain, in *The Alphabet versus the Goddess*, the Greeks also saw him as the god of the moon, night, altered states of consciousness, and the sensual celebration of dance and music. He was the god of the lucky hunch, the flash of insight, and intuitive knowledge. He taught mortals how to cultivate the grapevine and then how to ferment the grapes into wine. While Dionysus was the god who brings man joy, he was also the suffering and dying god whose death holds out the promise of salvation through rebirth. He was the god of tragic contrast. But most important, he was the god of the irrational and the unexplainable.

Shlain tells us "madness is the extreme irrationality." However, archaic peoples considered irrationality coequal with reason. Unlike our world that honors only the rational, the ancients considered irrationality to be as important as reason. It's interesting that the Greeks who honored logic so highly gave madness such a valued place of honor. When Dionysus arrived on the scene, madness took over, and all tradition, all order was shattered. Dionysus takes us from ecstasy to terror with amazing swiftness.

In the ancient world of the Great Goddess, altered states of consciousness were highly valued and common. In that world, irrationality in its different forms of prophecy, intuition, and altered states of consciousness, were associated with the goddess and revered. Drugs were frequently used to achieve an altered state of consciousness which encouraged a sense of revelation, possession and trance. Evidence indicates that the ancient Greeks did the same. Among the ancient (from the second millennium BCE) Minoan artifacts I saw in Crete at the Heraklion Museum, was a figurine of the goddess wearing a crown of three poppy seed-heads cut as for the extraction of opium. There also was an ancient seal showing the seated goddess holding three poppy seed-heads. In the Greek world, growing opium poppies has a very long history.

Plutarch, the Greek essayist and biographer, wrote that the worship of Dionysus among country folk was an occasion for rural merrymaking. The Dionysian cult believed getting drunk was a holy thing to do—it symbolically liberated the soul from the body, which allowed the god to enter and take possession of the worshiper—so their cultic activities were probably quite loose.

Given the viewpoint that drugs and wine helped make the religious experiences more intense, it is easy to see how wild and frenzied dancing became a major part of the cult of Dionysus. His women followers called the Bacchantes or Maenads (mad women) became intoxicated by chewing ivy leaves and eating of the hallucinogenic drug we know as psylocybin, which they called "the body of Dionysus." They performed their rites on mountaintops at the dark of the moon. Legend tells us they would tear to pieces any man who happened to cross their path or enter their sacred precincts. I saw Euripides's play *The Bacchae* some years ago and, in the play, this is exactly what the women did. The amount of destruction Dionysus could inflict on those who did not honor his presence was truly awesome. There is nothing like a 2,500-year-old play to reduce the audience to sheer terror.

As in all ancient religions, sacrifices were very important. For the cult of Dionysus, the goat was the major offering. The he-goat is one of the most loyal associates of the god Dionysus. As Plutarch describes the processions during the celebrations of Dionysus, the wine jar came first, then a vine stock, a he-goat, a basket of figs, and finally the phallus. The he-goat symbolizes the powers of procreation, the life force, the libido and fertility. Otto tells us Dionysus himself was called "the young kid," because of his close relation to the goat. In myth too, Dionysus appears in goat form at times. The he-goat was also favored as a sacrificial victim to Dionysus. Tragedy in Greek means "goat-song" and it originally referred to the sacrifice of a goat in vegetation and fertility rituals associated with the god Dionysus, in whose honor tragedies were performed. As Harrison says, from the religion of Dionysus sprang the drama.

Dionysus was the deity not only of revels and abandon but also of festivals and spectacles in general, of poetic inspiration, and through his ceremonies, the founder of Greek drama. Drama is the art form that combines poetry, music, gesture, and spectacle. Tragedy is a branch of drama that treats in a serious and dignified style the sorrowful or terrible events a heroic individual encounters or causes. Scholars suggest that the starkly universal themes of tragedy, the problems and conditions of life lived under the shadow of death and disaster, may be connected with the seasonal rhythms of life, decay, death, and rebirth.

Drama started as a rural religious service held in December at the festivals of Dionysus. According to Harrison, the choral lyric called the dithyramb is actually a birth-song. It celebrated the rebirth of nature, spring's awakening in the person of the infant god, and was used in the religious service by the Greeks of Greece proper and those of South Italy and Sicily. The dithyramb was not the outpouring of an individual inspired singer, but rather a choric dance, the dance and song of a band. This type of group spring-song of magical fertility was very old and dated back to the days of worship of the Great Goddess and her son. The religious ritual was designed to make sure the deities brought spring after winter.

The chanted dithyrambs included dances, leaping and some mimicry. Jane Harrison, in *Themis: A Study of the Social Origins of Greek Religion*, states the dancers must have been part of the initiation rites for youths, who danced in an excited type of war-dance, rain-dance, or thunder-dance. The dancers, dancing together, utter their joint desire, delight, and terror, in steps and gestures, in cries of fear or joy or lamentation, in shrieks of war. This made the experience more intense. A group experience such as this feels larger than the experience of the individual. The dancers themselves try to heighten this effect. They do this by submerging their own personality, by the wearing of masks and disguises, by dancing to a common rhythm, and above all by the common excitement; they become emotionally one and not a collection of individuals. The emotion they feel collectively, the thing that is greater than any individual emotion, is the structure of worship.

The primitive past from the days of Great Goddess worship shaped the basic form and structure of the Greek drama. The pattern of the ritual became the structure of the drama, and its different rites and ceremonies became the acts and scenes. According to Theodore Gaster in *Thespis* the farther back in history we go, the more likely we are to find in the original design such ancient ritual rites from the period of the Goddess as the Sacred Marriage, the Feast of Communion, and the Expulsion of Evil—all of them disguised, of course, and duly woven into the plot. Recent studies of classical Greek tragedy and comedy make this clear. Greek drama was an exploration of human faults, passions, and excesses that dealt with the irony of fate, and the justice (or injustices) of the gods. It tells of heroes consumed by hubris.

The first actors to perform on a stage covered their faces with huge masks exaggerating each character's expression. The twin masks of tragedy and comedy that, to us, symbolize the theater, can be traced back to the worship of Dionysus, who represented the duality in human nature. While Greek vase painters often depicted the faces of all the other gods in profile, Dionysus was the one they represented frontally. Because it is his nature to appear suddenly and with overwhelming might before mankind, the mask serves as his symbol. He was the god of confrontation—the god who startled. The mask, which was always a sacred object, could also be put on over a human face to depict the god or spirit that appears. The idea of Dionysus has been there in celebrating maskers up through the Renaissance, and lives on today in the masked revelers of Mardi Gras and Halloween.

The village folk-plays, still performed in Northern Greece and elsewhere at carnival time, to this day still keep all these distinctive features of the original design. Levy tells us in these, as in the most primitive initiation legends, the hero is always strangely born, taken from his mother, killed, and restored to life; this is a series of events which would equally fit a passion play of Dionysus. But these folk-plays contain further elements which relate them to an older series of vegetation cults, such as a fight in which the hero is killed, usually at his marriage feast, by a double who often wears an animal skin or mask, or has a blackened face. After the mourning and resurrection, his interrupted wedding is fulfilled amid general rejoicing followed by revelry. This type of play belongs to the New Year rites that, in Western Asia, inaugurated the New Year.

In time, the choral lyrics in honor of the god developed into a series of exchanges between the chorus and its leader. By about 500 BCE the choral lyric had developed into a series of exchanges between the chorus, its leader, the *tragodos*, and another man who was known as "the answerer," or *hypokrites*, the word from which comes "hypocrite," one who plays a part. Hypokrites, came to be the Greek word for actor.

By the middle of the sixth century BCE the dithyramb which they were chanting developed to a real art form. Choosing a leader for the chorus was a major step in the development of the drama form. Now by having a chief dancer as a spokesman the role, in time, became larger. As time went on and the leader's role became larger, the chorus became spectators.

During the 560's to the 530's BCE, Athens became the spiritual center of the settlements grouped around it. Hale tells us it was during this time the annual rural festivals to the nature god Dionysus, with their choral chants and dances, were brought to Athens. Finally, out of these festivals, there grew the rudimentary art of the drama. Tragedy was always connected with the worship of Dionysus. The first public contest for a tragic play was set up in Athens in the year 534 BCE—and with this event the history of the Greek theater begins. As urban life grew people became less dependent on the cycles of the year. When that happened, the traditional ceremonies, which connected the people to the land and the cycles of the year, lost their urgency and the myth became dominant. Dramatic ritual then became drama proper.

At the Dionysian festival in Athens, the first day had a ceremonial re-entry of the god into Athens, escorted by a torchlight procession. The next morning there was a great parade, which took sacrifices and gifts to his temple. In the afternoon there was a choral contest among the entries. That night there was a *komos*, or revel, at which there was a good deal of drinking and gaiety that often became riotous.

Other days were given over to the performance of tragedies and comedies in the Theater of Dionysus. The priest of Dionysus, flanked by other priests, sat in the front row. The performances, which lasted all day, were taken with high seriousness. Even the comedies, gay and bawdy as they generally were, were far from being mere frothy amusement, for they commented on serious matter in the comic spirit.

Authors who wished to present tragedies submitted them to an official chosen to select the plays. After due deliberation, three of these writers were told that this official would "give them a chorus." The author would train the chorus himself, at least in the early days; later there were professional trainers. In these early times the writer himself took the part of *tragodos*, the person who talked with the chorus and led it.

According to Levy in time the two choirs of "answerers" in the Athenian festival seem to have been replaced by the second and third actor. Now the action could be moved away from the chorus to between the actors so the plot could be developed. The chorus was still essential, since the religious source of drama required the presence of an audience already sympathetically identified with the action.

The strange thing about tragedy is that while awful things happen in plays such as *Antigone* and *Hamlet*—at the end corpses are littering the stage—instead of being depressed or horrified, most of us are exhilarated by the experience. Pity, awe, reconciliation, and exaltation—these are the elements that make up tragic pleasure. But when we speak of tragedy we tend to use more uplifting language. We always go to the height of tragedy. Joseph Campbell in *Hero with a Thousand Faces*, tells us that the "purification" or "purgation" of the emotions of the spectator of tragedy through his experience corresponds to an earlier ritual *katharsis* ("a purification of the community from the taints and poisons of the past year, the old contagion of sin and death") which was the function of the festival and mystery play of dismembered god, Dionysos.

Though few temples were ever erected to Dionysus, the great Greek playwrights, Aeschylus, Euripides, and Sophocles built the greatest of shrines to him when they wrote their dramas for performance at his festivals. These are among the greatest dramas ever written in which the celebration of human joy and fulfillment were mixed with recognition of the tragic condition of man. When I followed the process through, it seemed natural that tragedy developed within the cult of Dionysus. Somehow in the midst of celebrating a religious rite to a long ago pagan god the ancient Greeks captured an emotion that today still stirs and satisfies us.

FOR FURTHER READING

Campbell, Joseph. *The Hero with a Thousand Faces*. Princeton, NJ: Bollingen Series, Princeton University Press, 1949. Print.
Chevalier, Jean, and Gheerbrant, Alain. *A Dictionary of Symbols*. New York: Penguin, 1944. Print.
Gaster, Theodore, H. *Thespis*. New York: Gordian Press, 1975. Print.
Godwin, Joscelyn. *Mystery Religions in the Ancient World*. San Francisco: HarperSanFrancisco, 1981. Print.
Graves, Robert. *The White Goddess*. New York: HarperCollins, 1966. Print.
Hale, William Harlan. *Ancient Greece*. New York: American Heritage Press, 1970. Print.

Hamilton, Edith. *The Greek Way to Western Civilization.* New York: Norton, 1993. Print.
Harrison, Jane Ellen. *Themis, A Study of the Social Origins of Greek Religion.* New Hyde Park, NY: University Books, 1962. Print.
Hawkes, Jacquetta. *Dawn of the Gods.* New York: Random House, 1968. Print.
Kerenyi, Carl. *Dionysos, Archetypal Image of Indestructible Life.* Princeton, NJ: Princeton University Press, 1976. Print.
Levy, Gertrude Rachel. *The Gate of Horn.* London: Faber & Faber, 1946. Print.
Otto, Walter. *Dionysus, Myth & Cult.* Dallas, TX: Spring Publication, 1981. Print.
Shlain, Leonard. *The Alphabet versus the Goddess: The Conflict Between Word and Image.* New York: Viking, 1998. Print.
Sjoo, Monica, and Mor, Barbara. *The Great Cosmic Mother.* New York: Harper & Row, 1987. Print.
Walker, Barbara. *The Woman's Dictionary of Symbols & Sacred Objects.* San Francisco: HarperSanFrancisco, 1988. Print.

CHAPTER 20

Water

STANDING IN THE LOBBY OF THE ATLANTIC CITY CASINO, I was fascinated by the coins in the fountain. Wishing for good luck at a casino by throwing coins in the fountain seemed a bit odd to me. I guess a gambler takes his good luck rituals wherever he can find them; but how did the idea develop of getting good luck from throwing coins in a fountain? I always thought it was the coins that brought the "good luck." When I began to study the issue more, I realized I had it backwards. The luck comes from the water; the coins are just an offering.

Many cults and rites throughout history are connected with various springs, streams and rivers that correspond to the many different values given to water. Mircea Eliade, in *Patterns in Comparative Religions*, says water flows, it is "living. By their very nature, spring and river display power, life, perpetual renewal; they are and they are alive. This quality of moving water has kept water's sacred quality alive in spite of the development of other religious beliefs."

There are many legends and stories of someone finding water from a rock or a spring from the earth by striking the place with a rod. Probably the best-known example is the example of Moses told in Numbers 20:11. But others are also told. Rhea needed water to bathe the newborn Zeus, so she struck the mountain and a stream gushed forth. Poseidon struck his trident to give rise to the Fountain of Lerna. These are only two other examples.

We know water is essential for life and growth. Also I knew, as most of us at some level do, that water is important in many of our cultural and religious rituals; but I really wasn't aware of the large role water played. Mircea Eliade in *Patterns in Comparative Religions*, tells us that in most religions, from ancient times to the present, spiritual purification rituals and ceremonies of rites of passage are symbolically marked by water. Among the most ancient people, water was considered the source of life, the medium of birth, death, and immortality, and the center of wisdom. Researchers have found examples of water worship in most of the major civilizations of the world, including ancient Egypt, classical Greece, Troy, Babylon and ancient Rome.

Water is still important in religion. For example, Ellen Frankel and Betsy Platkin Teutsch in *The Encyclopedia of Jewish Symbols* tell us Judaism has many water themes in its fall holiday cycle. The Torah reading on Rosh Hashanah, the New Year holiday, includes the story of the miraculous well that saved Hagar and Ishmael in the wilderness. On Rosh Hashanah afternoon, traditional Jews go to a river or stream to perform the ceremony of "Tashlikh" (Casting) where they cast off their sins by throwing breadcrumbs into the water. On Yom Kippur, the Day of Atonement, the Book of Jonah with the story of the whale is recited. During the ancient days of the Temple a special festival called the "Rejoicing of the House of Water-Drawing" was celebrated during Sukkot. It included pouring out water libations, singing, shofar blowing and dancing.

To the people of pre-history, water symbolized the Great Mother with both her life-giving and death-bringing aspects. Barbara Walker in *The Woman's Encyclopedia of Myths and Secrets* tells us sanctuaries dedicated to the Goddess usually included a spring or some course of water. When you think of the earth as the body of the Great Mother as the ancients did, the well or spring symbolized her womb, therefore it had a special significance for birth and children. Immersion in such sacred water purifies and regenerates. This is how water acquired the quality of being a miraculous healer.

There were also other kinds of rites connecting the ancient goddess and the sea. I was really surprised some summers ago to see the mayor of Atlantic City, New Jersey, on the news sailing a small boat into the ocean to drop a wedding ring in the sea. The news commentator said this was an old custom of many seaside cities where, annually, there is a celebration in which the city is married to the sea. Certainly this was true in olden days. In the Middle Ages the rulers of Venice, the Doges, celebrated an annual marriage to the Sea Goddess every year on Ascension Day, by throwing into the sea "a gold ring of great value." Also the main staircase in the Winter Palace of St. Petersburg was special because at Epiphany the Czars descended these steps on their way to consecrate the Neva River. Atlantic City obviously is continuing an old idea. Somehow I don't think a serious religious rite is a factor.

In ancient days and now, water was known to be closely tied to the moon because of the tides. The Moon Mother was another central feminine symbol. Esther Harding in *Woman's Mysteries* tells us that the shrines of the Moon Mother were usually in groves where there was a spring; often they were in a grotto where the water trickled directly out of the rock.

Harding tells us in her role as giver of rain, the moon deity is quite unaccountable; for not only does she send rain in the spring, when it is needed for the young crops, but she also sent storms in August that frequently destroyed the very harvest she generously gave. For this reason in ancient days, special rites were held to convince the goddess not to send these harvest storms. On the thirteenth of August in Greece there was a great festival in honor of Hecate, the moon goddess; and in Rome, of Diana, Hecate's direct descendant. On this day the Goddess's aid was called upon to avert the storms that might hurt the coming harvest.

Ceremonies of water drawing and pouring were a constant feature of service to the goddess. The water was poured out to remind the goddess to send rain. In addition, the ancients felt the pouring out of the water strengthened the goddess's powers.

For the ancients, water was the source both of life and of death, which makes water both creator and destroyer. This idea, according to Mircea Eliade in *Images and Symbols,* is expressed by the ancient Moon Goddess, who as the life giver of all living things is also the destroyer. According to the ancients, floods are her favorite tool of destruction. She is the cause of rain and storm and tide as well as flood. It is she who creates all life on the earth but then she creates the flood, which destroys the life she created. But she laments what she did and does her best to save her children. According to Esther Harding, in *Woman's Mysteries, Ancient and Modern,* in the Babylonian account of the great flood, Ishtar the Moon Goddess causes the great flood and then saves some of her people from the flood she brought. Many scholars believe the Old Testament story of the flood is derived from the more ancient tale from Babylonia. Noah, in the Old Testament story, is probably a form of Nuah, a Babylonian moon goddess. Like Ishtar, Noah saved a remnant of the world in an ark that he built. Then when the waters receded, Noah, advised by a dove, a bird always associated with moon deities, came out onto the land. Ishtar, in the Babylonian story, also chose a dove as her messenger.

Moon goddesses from various regions were regarded as guardians of the water, rivers, brooks, and springs. These usually were considered sacred to the goddess of fertility. According to Jean Markale in *The Great Goddess,* the tradition continues to this day with most of the churches and chapels dedicated to the Virgin Mary having a fountain or an inside well, for example at Chartres, or a spring, or a fountain or well nearby.

According to Eliade the power for water to purify and regenerate comes because the ancients believed water could wipe out the past. Such washing made people new again. It purified man from crime, from the unlucky presence of the dead, from madness; it destroyed sins and stopped the process of mental or physical decay. Water rituals occur before all major religious acts, to prepare man for his coming into the realm of the sacred. One always washed before going into temples and before sacrifices.

Water is widespread as an instrument of ritual purification. In this respect, washing plays an important role in traditions from all over the ancient world. In India and Southeast Asia statues of the gods—as well as the worshipers themselves—are regularly washed (especially at New Year) as a rite both of cleansing and of regeneration.

Eliade tells us that the sacred ceremonial baths of the statues of the divinities were generally performed in the cult of the Great Goddesses of fertility and agriculture. The ancients felt this strengthened the goddess's flagging powers, and by their doing this they were ensuring a good harvest (immersion as a magic rite was supposed to produce rain) and an increase in goods. The statues of the great Greek goddesses (such as Hera, for example) were bathed each year in order to regenerate their immortal powers, especially their virginity (a symbol of their creative potential). Aphrodite, too, often is shown rising up out of the waters.

For traditional Jews, according to Frankel and Platkin, immersion in the mikvah brings about spiritual purification, not physical cleanliness. This is one of the most ancient rituals in Jewish life which usually is translated as "ritual bath," but actually it is identical to the word used in Genesis to describe the primeval "gathering of the waters" (Genesis 1:10). The mikvah is either a natural water source, such as a spring, lake, or stream, or an artificial pool containing freely flowing rain or spring water. One of the uses of the mikvah is to have it as part of the ritual which welcomes "new-born" Jews—converts and non-Jewish adopted children into the community.

In Christianity, water baptism is a chief instrument of spiritual regeneration. But baptism is not limited to the Jewish and Christian traditions; numerous other religions have ablution rites.

In Knossos, in Crete, where the enormous works of the Minoans have been uncovered, there is what archeologists call a "throne room." Across the room and down several steps is something called a "lustral basin." My husband insists it's an early mikvah as it meets the traditional requirements for one. Regardless, it was used for ritual purposes that somehow involved a ritual of cleansing and renewal. As I said before the ancients felt that such an act regenerated the vital forces of the goddess.

In Indian tradition the Ganges, like the Jordan in Judeo-Christian tradition, is a sacred river. It is called Mother Ganges, and she is both a river and the goddess Gangadevi. Her waters are said to be capable of bestowing immortality. The famous Indian festival called the Kumbha Mela is held four times every twelve years rotating among four locations on the Ganges River: Allahabad, Haridwar, Ujjain and Nashik. Millions and millions of people come at that time to bathe in the sacred water of the Ganges. The devout believe deeply in its powers. It is said that if one bathes in the Ganges or even sprinkles three drops of Ganges water on his head, he becomes freed from past sins.

The places in the earth where water erupted to the surface—springs and wells—as well as lakes and rivers, according to Bord, were particular spots of reverence. The reverence took many forms, including the performing of rituals and the leaving of gifts. The finding of a spring close to an ancient or sacred site may have sanctified it in the eyes of the local people, since water welling up from the earth at a sacred site would naturally be considered to possess great potency. The use of water from wells and springs has from the earliest times been closely linked with various religious practices, and as a result has acquired all manner of symbolism and ritual.

The Romans considered water an important aspect of their religious practices. This is shown by the number of their temples located at wells or close to a water source. Some were beside rivers; others had springs, wells, or ponds close by. When the water source was inside the temple itself, it clearly was the focal point of the religious practices.

The ancients believed strongly in the healing powers of water. When I visited the hot spring at Bath, England, I was suffering acutely from degenerative arthritic hips: only soaking in hot water gave temporary relief. Seeing the steaming waters there gave me a whole new insight into how miraculous a hot spring that provided such relief must have felt to the ancients. The deity of the hot spring at Bath was the native goddess Sulis, who was linked to the classical Roman goddess Minerva. Her nearby temple was a healing center. Another example of a water-healing center is Lourdes in Southwestern France where, in 1858, it is believed that the Virgin Mary appeared to a peasant girl. Many pilgrims come to the place of the vision to bathe in the sacred water of the grotto spring in hopes that a miracle will restore them to health. Interestingly, in the 8th century before Lourdes was called Lourdes it was called Puy and was home to the Black Virgin of Puy.

A healing function is part of most of the holy wells in Britain and Ireland. Wells were also a point of contact with the underworld and its supernatural beings. When the wells and springs were adopted by the Christians and became dedicated to the saints, these beings became absorbed into the lore along with the spirits and goddesses of paganism. Most churches and chapels dedicated to the Virgin Mary included a fountain or a well. As time went on, many of the ancient customs were included in the Christian tradition.

In Britain, before and even after the Romans and their influence left, belief in the healing powers of the wells persisted. Janet and Colin Bord in *Sacred Waters: Holy Wells and Water Lore in Britain & Ireland*, tell us during the following centuries the water cult spread until there were thousands of sacred wells throughout Britain, each with pilgrims who vouched for the potency of their well. Up to the twelfth century, edicts banning water worship were still being issued, but gradually, as the influence of Christianity spread across the land, the old customs were overlaid by Christian observances. Since water is used in Christian rituals for baptism and hand washing, it was easy to adopt the well water for these purposes. Baptisteries were built at wells, and churches were built close to, or even over, wells.

Water was also used to mark a sacred area. A way of marking such an area was to encircle it. In mythology and fairy tales, magic castles are surrounded by a circular moat, or a rushing stream. No magic rite can safely occur unless first a protective circle is drawn around it. Such protection can be given by a "blind spring," which is a spot from which a number of underground streams flow, forming a radiating pattern of energy. According to Monica Sjoo and Barbara Mor in *The Great Cosmic Mother*, to the ancients, the blind spring was the center, both spiritually as well as physically, of its sacred monuments. It was "holy" (healing) ground, a place of harmonious power where the Goddess dwelt. Blind springs were found at the center of the most ancient temples, as well as the medieval churches of Britain and Europe. Gates of cities and temples were also set over blind springs, giving "divine protection" to those entering and leaving. Holy, healing, and oracular wells were sunk on blind springs, and the most ancient cities of the

Near East, such as Jericho and Catal Huyuk, Turkey, were built over such sacred wells.

Wells are symbols of plenty and sources of life. In the *Zohar*, a Jewish medieval text, a well fed by a stream symbolizes the marriage of man and woman. In Hebrew the word "well" carries the meaning of "woman" or "bride." Biblical women are often linked with wells, especially Rebecca and Miriam. Because of the numerous associations of wells and women, Jewish feminists have incorporated water in many contemporary rituals, especially those that celebrate Rosh Hodesh (the festival of the New Moon) and to mark rites of passage.

Miriam, the sister of Moses and Aaron, was one of the leaders of the Jewish people both in Egypt and in the wilderness. In recent times, Miriam has become a prominent symbol for Jewish feminists of Jewish women's political and spiritual leadership. Frankel and Teutsch tell us that Jewish legend claims that at twilight on the Sixth Day of Creation, God created a miraculous well, which because of Miriam's merits, accompanied the Children of Israel in their wanderings, and disappeared at her death. The folk tradition says that Miriam's Well fills all wells at the end of Shabbat and gives such water curative powers. Recently it has become popular to put a glass of water on the Seder table at Passover to remember Miriam. In Hebrew, the word for well is the same as the verbal root, "to understand." Wells have often been traditional symbols of wisdom.

A pilgrim's final act before leaving a holy well was usually to leave some object in or by the well, and these objects are generally regarded as gifts or offerings. According to Bord, the most popular "offering" was a pin, usually bent. Another popular offering were rags tied to a nearby bush. No one is quite sure why bent pins were favored, and why rags were tied to bushes. The custom of throwing gifts or offerings into wells continued into Roman times, objects having been found in a number of Roman wells in Britain. The tradition never stopped. In early times, large and valuable offerings were thrown into lakes and rivers. Beautiful examples of Celtic craftsmanship, such as shields and lunulae (crescent-shaped gold ornaments) have been found in the rivers of Britain. Hoards of metalwork found in lakes or buried in once water-covered areas attest strongly to the existence of water cults.

As the centuries passed and religious beliefs changed, in many areas the sacred wells were less honored and pilgrims no longer approached them with such feelings of devotion. In time, people stopped offering prayers to the saint of the wells, instead they made a wish. This is how we got our "wishing wells" including the one in the casino. Water as a symbol has always been popular with the people. Think about this the next time you toss a coin into a wishing well.

FOR FURTHER READING

Bord, Janet and Colin. *Sacred Waters: Holy Wells and Water Lore in Britain & Ireland.* London: Granada, 1985. Print.

Chevalier, Jean, and Gheerbrant, Alain. *A Dictionary of Symbols.* New York: Penguin, 1944. Print.

Cirlot, J. E. *A Dictionary of Symbols.* New York: Philosophical Library, Inc., 1962. Print.

Eliade, Mircea. *Patterns in Comparative Religion.* Translated: R. Sheed. London: Sheed and Ward, 1958. Republished Lincoln, NE: University of Nebraska Press, 1996. Print.

———. *The Sacred and the Profane: The Nature of Religion.* Translated from French: W. R. Trask. New York: Harvest/HBJ Publishers, 1957. Print.

———. *Images and Symbols: Studies in Religious Symbolism.* Translated: P. Mairet. London: Harvill Press, 1961. Print.

Frankel, Ellen, and Teutsch, Betsy Platkin. *The Encyclopedia of Jewish Symbols.* Northvale, NJ: Jason Aronson Inc., 1992. Print.

Gaster, Theodore H. *Myth, Legend and Custom in the Old Testament.* New York: Harper Torchbooks, 1975. Print.

Harding, M. Esther. *Woman's Mysteries, Ancient & Modern.* Boston: Shambala Publications, 1990. Print.

Jones, Prudence, and Pennick, Nigel. *A History of Pagan Europe*. New York and London: Routledge, 1995. Print.

Markale, Jean. *The Great Goddess*. Rochester, VT: Inner Tradition, 1997. Print.

Moon, Beverly, Ed. *An Encyclopedia of Archetypal Symbolism*. Boston: Shambala Publications, 1991. Print.

Neumann, Erich. *The Great Mother*. Princeton, NJ: Princeton University Press, 1974. Print.

Sjoo, Monica, and Mor, Barbara. *The Great Cosmic Mother*. New York: Harper & Row, 1987. Print.

Walker, Barbara. *The Woman's Dictionary of Symbols & Sacred Objects*. San Francisco: HarperSanFrancisco, 1988. Print.

CHAPTER 21

The Dawning of the Age of Aquarius

DO YOU REMEMBER THE 1960S HIT MUSICAL SHOW "Hair"? One of its most popular songs was "The Dawning of the Age of Aquarius." The whole idea of this song fascinated me. Exactly what was an Age and how did Aquarius, a sign of the Zodiac, get into it, and why was it "dawning"? About that time people started using the term "New Age." Was that the same thing? If so, when can we expect it? What will it bring? How will things change? I found the answers to this much more complicated than I thought. They are a combination of straight astronomy, considerable astrology, much mythology and a fair amount of Jungian psychology. Don't laugh; while the story is strange, I find it fascinating.

The whole process of the idea of Ages of the Zodiac is created by an astronomical event called "Precession." We all know the earth revolves around the sun; a year is a complete orbit, and each rotation of the earth around its own axis is a day. But there is a movement of the earth as it revolves around the sun. It is called precession, which few of us ever think about.

As Robert Bauvel and Adrian Gilbert in *The Orion Mystery* explain, the easiest way to describe precession is to think of the earth as a spinning top which, like a top as it turns, has a wobble. The precession of the earth, its wobble as it revolves, is caused by the gravitational pull of the moon and the sun on the earth's equatorial bulge. The complete wobble on a top takes seconds, but the complete wobble of the earth as it travels around the sun takes 26,000 years to do. It takes that long for the axis created by the earth's pole to circle the zodiac of the sky and so complete one wobble. This 26,000-year period is called a Great Year. The Great Year then gets divided into twelve ages, each age being about 2,300 years long.

Each age is defined by a group of stars called a constellation. A constellation of stars is like a picture in the sky, the stars in it create its shape. Some of the constellations are large, some are small; some have several bright stars, some have none. The constellation's shape affects the size and the length of the time it takes earth to travel through it. Each constellation has a story of some ancient myth attached to it. From the myth the constellation has a name like Aries or Taurus.

The twelve constellations or patterns in the sky, called the Zodiac, form a band around the horizon of the sky, called the ecliptic. While we know the earth revolves around the sun, when we look at the sky it really seems as if the sun is revolving around the earth; and in the course of the year, it seems the sun is rising and setting in each of the twelve constellations of the Zodiac.

Twice a year, at the time of the spring and fall equinoxes (the days when day and night are each 12 hours long), the earth's axis is tilted exactly sideways to the sun. As Demetra George in *The Mysteries of the Dark Moon*, explains it, one equinox takes place on September 21 and is the start of autumn, the other, called the vernal equinox, marks the start of spring on March 21. The age we are in is marked by the star constellation which is the backdrop for the rising sun on the morning of the vernal equinox. It happens that after 2,300 years or so, the rising sun, on the day of the vernal equinox shows the sun rising in a different constellation. This changes the sky, the stars no longer rise at their right time, and the whole sky has shifted. Because the vernal equinox moves westward, Demetra tells us we are now in Pisces moving into Aquarius, which is how we get to the "Age of Aquarius."

The astrologers tell us that when we move into a different age, not only has the real sky changed, but also according to them, the whole pattern of life on earth in some way changes. Alan Oken in *Complete Astrology* explains that each of the ages created by precession has a different political and sociological structure as well as a different consciousness. Most of the ancient religions of the earth were based on observation of the sky, so historians feel that reconstruction of the ancient sky helps us to learn not only why the ancients created their temples and monuments the way they did, but also helps explain their symbols and myths.

Many in the modern world think astrology is silly. Modern science makes astrology part of the occult. However, despite all efforts to debunk it, people still to some degree believe that someone's sign can tell the personality of a person, as well as predicting the future by examining the movement of the stars.

Leonard Shlain, in *The Alphabet versus the Goddess: The Conflict Between Word and Image*, tells us that, in ancient days, astrologers were often very important people. Every court had an official astrologer who advised the monarch. Commanders canceled entire military campaigns if the alignment of the stars was unfavorable. Common people, coping with the difficulties of daily life, found it helpful to consult astrologers. Marriages were arranged, and in certain cultures still are, by the compatibility of the signs of the bride and groom.

Now this is where the idea of the Great Year really gets strange. Shlain tells us the astrologers believe that everything is determined by the stars. Therefore, the sun, at the time of the vernal equinox, passes from rising in one constellation to rise in another one, and the symbolism associated with the old constellation gives way to that of the new. In other words, according to Alice O. Howell in *Jungian Synchronicity in Astrological Signs and Ages*, the astrologers believe that just as a person's personality is determined by the stars, so is the "personality" of the age. This idea shows up in the religious and cultural images of that world age. Therefore, the old mythology which explained the world for the ancients of the last age no longer works, and a new mythology must be created. Astrologers say this happens because there is intelligent patterning in the universe. A Jungian would say it happened at the level of the collective unconscious, mysteriously and spontaneously, of its own accord.

These things, of course, do not happen overnight, but take place over several hundred years. This time is called the "cusp of the ages." According to Howell, cusp periods are always time of intense change where the old is dying in order to give birth to the new. It is important to remember that it takes a very long time for the sun to stop rising in one constellation and move to another. Even though you can't pinpoint the exact time when we enter a new age, things happen which indicate definite shifts in the collective unconsciousness of the period.

Okay, we have a new age dawning, one that will be with us for the next two thousand years. Before we look at what's coming, let's take a look at some past Ages and their beliefs, myths, and symbols. What does this concept of the Ages tell us about the evolution of human consciousness and the human psyche? Each age is different. Each has its own mythology, symbols and meanings. It makes no sense that they should, but somehow history and archeology tell us they do.

Let's start by taking a look at the Age of Cancer (circa 8000–6500 BCE). This is the time of the late Stone Age (Neolithic). According to Howell, although this is before the written word, we have lots of artifacts of this time from Anatolia, the Near

East and Europe. The artifacts show these ancients worshipped the Great Mother. The "Venus" figures of this time all have large breasts and hips. In this period the vagina of the Earth Mother who gave birth to her children and then took their bodies back into herself at death was the major motif. Cancer is associated with the archetype of the Great Mother and the process of bearing, birthing, nurturing, protecting.

After the Age of Cancer came the Age of Gemini (6500–3750 BCE). Remember we are moving backward through the zodiac. Howell tells us that, during this time, there was a new wave of human development, the beginning of the great shifting from the mother religions to the father religions—and with that, the development of the patriarchy. In the astrological world, the sign of Gemini is associated with all things dealing with communication: writing, reading, newspapers, books, making mental connections, and most importantly a sense of humor—fun, games, puns, riddles, etc. Besides the caduceus, among Gemini's symbols are the masks of tragedy and comedy and all examples of pairs of things or opposites. Gemini is also concerned with such opposites as mortal/immortal, animal/human, large/small and on and on. It is from the tension of opposites that all new things emerge. With writing, prehistory became history, and humans were now able to communicate across space as well as across time.

The next precessional age is that of Taurus (c. 4220 BCE–c. 2160 BCE) Taurus is the sign of the bull. Oken tells us this is the period in which major advances took place in farming, largely through the new ability to domesticate oxen. During the Age of Taurus the Bull, humanity worldwide honored the Holy Cow, the Golden Calf, and Heifer. Krishna appeared in India spreading the cult of the cow; the Semites worshiped the bull god El; and in Crete it was Europa, who as a cow gave birth to the Bull King Minos. Remember Europa? She was the one for whom Zeus, in order to seduce her, turned himself into a bull. This was a detail I never understood until I realized that, if you are going to seduce a cow (Europa), you need to be a bull. That story is a perfect example of the transition from worship of the female goddess to that of the male. The Great Goddess Hera was revered as the cow-eyed queen, Hathor as the celestial cow, and across the Mediterranean islands Cypress, Malta, and Sardinia, the peoples all practiced the cult of the cow and bull. According to George, the horns of the bull were seen to reflect the lunar crescent. As the moon is exalted in the sign of Taurus, the worship of the Neolithic Moon Goddess permeated the land during this world age.

The vernal equinox point continued its rotation and now began moving into the constellation of Aries the Ram in the middle of the third millennium BCE (c. 21,160 BCE–c. 1 CE). According to George, moving into the Age of Aries was depicted in the Old Testament when Moses went up to the mountaintop and saw the revelation of god in the burning bush (like Aries, a fiery sign). He then came down and proclaimed the change in world ages by blowing the ram's horn and warning people that they could no longer worship the Golden Calf, but instead must offer the sacrificial lamb to honor their God. The age of Aries was an age of warriors and thinkers. Differences between people became very important and clearly marked. The era was one of great aggressiveness and violence. This was the period of the Persian, Greek and Roman empires. The basic characteristic of the Age of Aries was a pioneering spirit, courage, distinct individuality, and an inner sense of truth and self-righteousness. During the Age of Aries, the focus of religious worship shifted. Bulls are now out and rams are in. The heroes are bull slayers.

The cult of the Ram spread to all parts of the civilized world. The names of many of the major deities were changed to illustrate the power of the cosmic forces at work in the new Age.

Mithra, the Sun god of Persia, who used to be called "The Sacred Bull," now became "The Slayer of the Bull." Ashur, Sun god of the Assyrians and known as "The Great Bull," was transformed into a Marslike god of war. George tells us Aries is related to the fire element and the fiery sun. During the Age of Aries, religious worship shifted from the moon mother goddesses to that of the father sun gods. This was the beginning of the end of the rule of the Mother Goddesses.

Given that ancient people believed astrology could predict the future, Shlain suggests how excited people must have been in the first century CE over a the passing from the Age of Aries to the coming of the Age of Pisces. It was at the time of the dawning of the age of Pisces (10 BCE–2000 CE) that Jesus was born. Maybe this was one of the reasons the new religion had so much appeal to the people of that time. In Christianity, the fish symbol is common. Yet before the dawning of the Age of Pisces, it was not a significant symbol in any of the prior major religions. Since the precessional movement takes place only every two thousand years or so, people must have been waiting, some with dread, some with hope. Soothsayers hawked their predictions and premonitions for the new Age of the Fish.

Christian associations with the fish are many. Howell tells us that the disciples were to be "fishers of men"; the Bishop's triangular hat is a fish head. Interestingly, the Virgin is usually symbolically depicted in the *vesica piscis*, the fish-like shape formed when two circles intersect. This is the ancient shape indicating the Goddess. Fish were eaten on Friday in honor of the goddess, a leftover from earlier goddess worshipping days. We still call a person who has difficulty relating a "cold fish." Christ's message of love, compassion, and surrender are all Piscean themes. However, George tells us that during this time these themes were not fully realized by the peoples of the earth. She feels this was partially due to the fact that the feminine principle continued to be dormant while the masculine energy proceeded to ascend unrestricted.

Now we find ourselves on the cusp or borderline between two world Ages, Pisces and Aquarius. This means that we have not quite left our former age nor are we yet completely in the new age. This is like leaving childhood and becoming a teenager. But one doesn't go to bed one night a child and wake the next day an adolescent; the process is gradual. So too, the world ages slowly merge one into the other. Thus today we find that we live in the legacy of Pisces and the promise of Aquarius.

Few astrologers agree about the dating of the dawn of this new Age, but Howell tells us Aquarian-type things started happening at the end of the 18th century. This was the time of the three great revolutions on behalf of the common man: the American, the French, and the Industrial Revolutions. Monarchies were toppled, and the cry was out for three famous Aquarian principles: Liberty, Brotherhood, and Equality. These are the cornerstones of the sign. While in the last two hundred years there have been many different political experiments such as communism, socialism, and democracy, we are still trying to find the best solution for representative government, without dictatorship, and a fair distribution of wealth and property, plus a guarantee of personal freedoms. The famous Four Freedoms (freedom of speech and worship, freedom from fear and want) are certainly Aquarian. We obviously are still working on them. But even the concept of a United Nations or a Common Market is a huge step in the right directions.

So what's coming? Well, that is the big question and one that astrology can certainly help answer. The astrologers point to the past eras and look to the characteristics of Aquarius to see what the next Age will bring us, both the good and the bad. There seems to be much conversation that says the Age of Aquarius will bring greater knowledge of the inner self as well as a greater involvement with the sacred.

Edward C. Whitmont in *Return of the Goddess* describes the images of Aquarius. He is the water carrier pictured as a male, and/or female divine guardian with an urn of water placed upon his/her shoulders. But the water of Aquarius refers not to ordinary, everyday water, but has a symbolic meaning. The Water Bearer signifies that Man has been created from the "waters" of life. In this respect the water is seen as the stream of universal consciousness, inspiration, and intuition. In the Age of Aquarius we can expect greater understanding of universal consciousness, inspiration and intuition.

Okens tells us that things are already beginning to happen as we approach the new age. We have developed many more uses for the air waves and many more are to come. In addition to radio, TV, telephone, and the like, we also have various forms of computer and satellite communication. Our minds must develop to deal with the new technology. My difficulty in doing that probably explains my distaste for any new devices coming on the market. Another example is that many people are realizing they have certain extrasensory gifts. The rising all over the world of "centers," "groups," and "communities" in which diverse ideas are exchanged is another example of what to expect in the Age of Aquarius.

Aquarians are associated with freedom, inventiveness, collective reform movements, and causes that are opposed to prejudice or narrow-mindedness in any form. No doubt this is why the various trends toward liberation in the 20th century are taken to indicate an Aquarian Age. But like everything else there is a shadow to the age. Aquarians are said to be like water, hard to pin down, erratic, subject to fits of unrest, and often shallow. According to Howell as a community down side there is too great detachment, too much emphasis on the collective, overlooking the individual. As our society reduces us more and more to ciphers and numbers this is something that is also of Aquarius. The highest suicide rates are in those countries where the government controls the security and welfare of all its citizens.

In many ways, it feels as if we have already entered the Age of Aquarius. We have the invention of mass production, global use of electricity, the car, phone, television, NASA, invention of technology to shrink the globe with computers, and satellite transmission of voice and data like the Internet. These are all related to Aquarius. The old structures of society such as the Church are becoming less influential in our spiritual lives as personal self-development becomes more important. This is a decline in the force of Pisces and the Great Religions.

Those who are discontented with our times are really awaiting the arrival of Aquarius. It can't come soon enough if you're tired of the Fish and figure something better is on the way. People who are particularly hopeful about the new age see a tidal wave of reform in its arrival. A more spiritual, loving, innovative, and progressive era is promised. The uncertainties and aggravations of our times are the "birth pangs" to the new age.

However, we have a long wait. The boundary between the constellations of Pisces and Aquarius adopted by the International Astronomical Union in 1928 delays the New Age border crossing until A.D. 2614 which gives us plenty of time to get ready. According to that, we have six centuries more before we move into a new era.

The Age of Aquarius will not bring a suddenly spiritually-oriented, love-sharing world population. We have a long way to go to work out our natural animal aggression. The road to peace is a long one. But we are beginning to realize how interconnected with each other we are. And Aquarius will be with us for quite a while, a bit more than two thousand years. So, starting from a world where the deity was female, moving through the world of the patriarchy, we now anticipate the arrival of Aquarius. Something new will surely develop. I'm sorry I won't be around to experience it.

FOR FURTHER READING

Bauval, Robert, and Gilbert, Adrian. *The Orion Mystery.* New York: Crown Publishers, 1994. Print.

George, Demetra. *Mysteries of the Dark Moon.* San Francisco: HarperSanFrancisco, 1992. Print.

Howell, Alice O. *Jungian Synchronicity in Astrological Signs and Ages.* Wheaton, IL: The Theosophical Publishing House, 1990. Print.

Huxley, Francis. *The Way of the Sacred.* New York: Doubleday & Co., 1974. Print.

Krupp, E. *Echoes of the Ancient Skies.* New York: Harper & Row, 1983. Print.

———. *Beyond the Blue Horizon.* Oxford, England: Oxford University Press, 1991. Print.

Mann, A. T. *Sacred Architecture.* New York: Barnes and Noble, 1993. Print.

Oken, Alan. *Complete Astrology.* New York: Bantam Books, 1988. Print.

Shlain, Leonard. *The Alphabet Versus the Goddess: The Conflict Between Word and Image.* New York: Viking, Penguin Group, 1998. Print.

Whitmont, Edward C. *Return of the Goddess.* New York: The Crossroad Publishing Co., 1992. Print.

IMAGE CREDITS

Page 6 (left): Photo © The London Art Archive / Alamy

Page 6 (right): Photo © The Print Collector / Alamy

Page 26: Photo © Israel Museum Jerusalem by Meidad Suchowolski

Page 55: Photo © The Print Collector / Alamy

Page 56: Photo © Louise Batalla Duran / Alamy

Page 59: Photo: Jill Brown / www.copix.co.uk

Page 70: Photo: The Metropolitan Museum of Art, Gift of Mrs. Russell Sage, 1908 (08.228)

Pages 71 and 122: Drawings by Miriam Seidel

Page 73: Photo © fotofacade.com / Alamy

Page 91: Photo © The London Art Archive / Alamy

Page 92: Photo: Collection Rijksmuseum, Amsterdam

Page 113: Photo © Tor Eigeland / Alamy

Page 117: Photo © Premier / Alamy

Page 167: Photo: The Metropolitan Museum of Art, Gift of Henry G. Marquand, 1897 (97.22.24).

Page 169: Photo: Cornell University Library

Page 172: Photo © JoeFox CountyMeath / Alamy

Page 173: Photo © Skyscan Photolibrary / Alamy

Page 180: Photo: Library of Congress, Gottscho-Schleisner Collection, LC-USZC2-4532.

ABOUT THE AUTHOR

 Annabel Lindy's original academic training was in science. After a short career as a chemist, she began a second career in banking and finance, working as a broker for Merrill Lynch. Then came her many years as a partner in her family's real estate business. Along the way, she developed a fascination with Goddess religions, stemming from her interest in feminism and women's rights. Through two decades of study and travel, she became an independent scholar of ancient modes of worship. *Her Story* is the culmination of that research, a distillation of her in-depth explorations.

www.ingramcontent.com/pod-product-compliance
Lightning Source LLC
Chambersburg PA
CBHW030232170426
43201CB00006B/190